CORNI
SEA STOR

◆

SHEILA BIRD

Illustrated by Jenny Fryatt

COUNTRYSIDE BOOKS
NEWBURY, BERKSHIRE

First published 1994

COUNTRYSIDE BOOKS
3, Catherine Road
Newbury, Berkshire

ISBN 1 85306 281 2

Cover illustration by Jenny Fryatt

Designed by Mon Mohan
Produced through MRM Associates Ltd., Reading
Typeset by Paragon Typesetters, Queensferry, Clwyd
Printed by J.W. Arrowsmith Ltd., Bristol

Also available

The Cornwall Village Book
Smuggling in the Bristol Channel 1700-1850
Smuggling in Devon and Cornwall 1700-1850
Tales of Old Cornwall

Contents

◆

N
W
S
Fire down Below!
Strange happenings at Godrevy
Fracas in St. Ives
The Mermaid of Zennor
Two Sail Standing Out
GODREVY ISLAND
ST. IVES
ZENNOR
HAYLE
PENDEEN WATCH
Sunken Land of Lyonesse
CAPE CORNWALL
ST. MICHAEL'S MOUNT
PENZANCE
NEWLYN
THE BRISONS
HELSTON
LONGSHIPS
LAND'S END
MOUNTS BAY
SEVEN STONES
A Navigational Catastrophe
The Capricious "Lady Daphne"
DOLLAR COVE
The Voyage of the "Mystery"
The Fate and Legacy of "H.M.S. Anson"
ISLES OF SCILLY

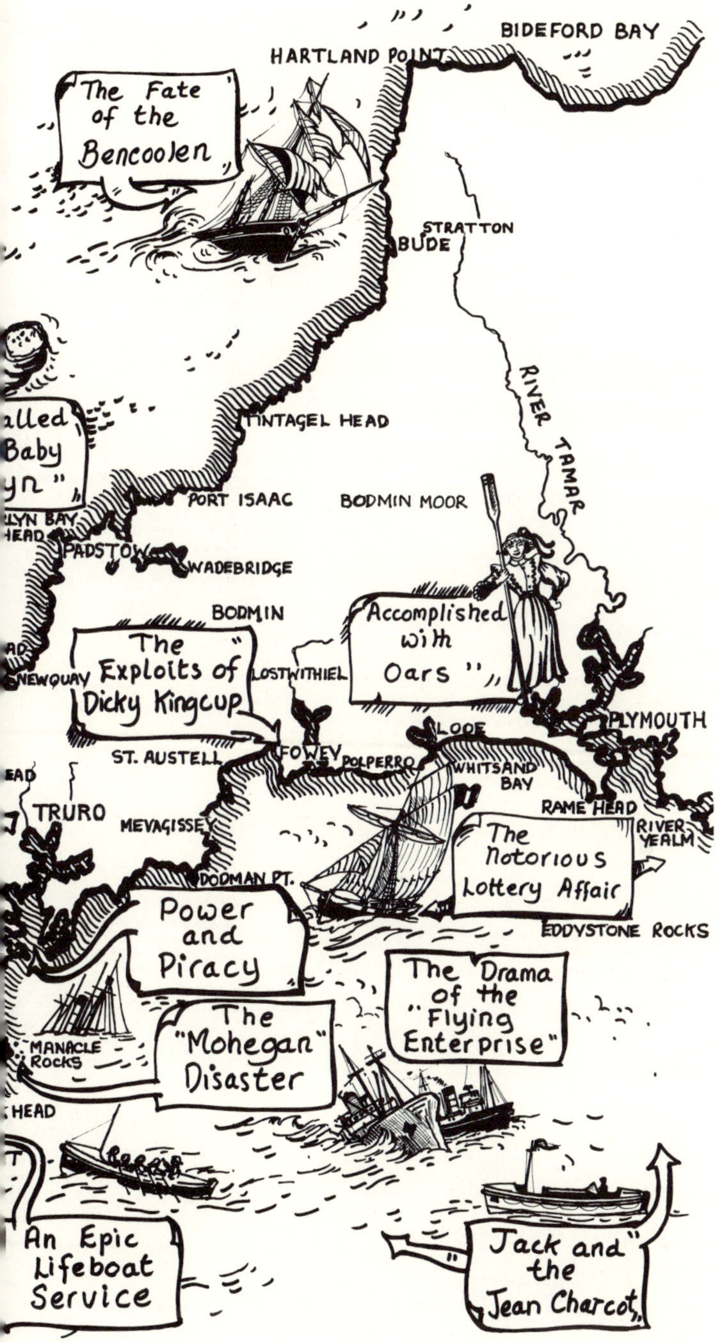

BIDEFORD BAY
HARTLAND POINT
The Fate of the Bencoolen
STRATTON
BUDE
RIVER TAMAR
TINTAGEL HEAD
alled Baby yn"
PORT ISAAC
BODMIN MOOR
PADSTOW
WADEBRIDGE
BODMIN
Accomplished with Oars"
The Exploits of Dicky Kingcup"
NEWQUAY
LOSTWITHIEL
LOOE
PLYMOUTH
ST. AUSTELL
FOWEY
POLPERRO
WHITSAND BAY
TRURO
MEVAGISSEY
RAME HEAD
The notorious Lottery Affair
RIVER YEALM
DODMAN PT.
Power and Piracy
EDDYSTONE ROCKS
The Drama of the "Flying Enterprise"
The "Mohegan" Disaster
MANACLE ROCKS
HEAD
An Epic Lifeboat Service
Jack and the Jean Charcot"

To Falmouth marine artist
Tony Warren,
recalling many happy hours of yarning, and in appreciation of all his help and encouragement in my early days as a writer.

1

'Two Sail Standing Out'

◆

'The Brisons are two rocky islets 90ft and 71ft high, lying W. by S. ¾S. half a mile from Cape Cornwall, and N.E. ⅞N. three and a half miles from the Longships. The N. islet is the higher. They must not be approached too near.'
(*Sailing Tours: Part 11: The Nore to the Scilly Isles, 1893*)

It was said at the time that the loss of a Government lighter was a very rare occurence, for naval workhorses of this type had to be of particularly robust construction, and were manned by proficient seamen. But in those grand and glorious days of sail, hazards came in various guises around the coast of Cornwall, particularly at the time of the spring and autumn equinox, and human error will be for ever with us.

Thirteen crewmen sailed on the Devonport Yard Craft No. 4 in the autumn of 1868, on a voyage destined to be beset by a series of misadventures and strange quirks of fate. As luck would have it, Davis, who had been the mate on this vessel was posted out to Gibraltar to serve aboard the paddle-wheel steam-tug *Redpole*, and it fell to his brother George, mate of the lighter *Hamoaze*, to take his place on this occasion. Having undergone a recent refit, the ill-fated, cutter-rigged lighter *Devon* left Devonport Dockyard on the morning of Tuesday, 21st October, under the command of Richard Helson, carrying a cargo of iron, ballast, cordage, chain cables, brooms, boats' oars, rum, tobacco and other Government stores, as well as the personal effects of some naval families, and she moved around to the Royal William Victualling Yard to take on provisions. Also aboard the ship as she set sail for Falmouth, Pembroke and Queenstown were two stewards returning to HMS *Revenge* at Pembroke, and the wife and two children of a Royal Marine serving aboard that ship, who were travelling as passengers.

The vessel was in fine trim as she set sail, but soon encountered heavy weather. She put into Falmouth at 1.20 am on the Thursday morning to carry out some work on a mooring buoy, and when she left the port nine hours later, the wind was blowing force 3, from NNW. It was freshening as they passed the Manacles at noon, and had increased to force 6, and veered W-by-S and WSW in the vicinity of the Lizard and Land's End, where sudden rain squalls and conflicting tides and currents added to the navigational problems and hampered their progress. Darkness had fallen and the squalls were becoming more violent by the time the mate, George Davis, took over from the captain at 8 pm. He proceeded to tack the vessel against the wind, which was strengthening to force 7, and kept the master informed of their progress and the state of the weather. It was hard going, but the vessel had cleared the south of Land's End and sighted the Longships Light at 9.45 pm. However, when Captain Helson reappeared on deck a couple of hours later, he expressed concern at their slow progress in regard to their bearings on the Longships, and drew attention to the barometer, which was falling fast. 'We're in for a fair ol' rollickin' this night, my boy,' he declared, and hurried below to put on his heavy weather gear before taking charge of the vessel. The wind was veering in these capricious conditions, and he altered course from NW to NNW, double-reefed the mainsail, then directed the helmsman to steer NNE. The vessel was shipping water in the heavy, confused seas.

The mate lingered on deck for a while, but when the chronometer was showing 1 am the master ordered him to go below and try and get some rest; for conditions, bad as they were, promised to deteriorate still further. As the young man turned to go, he noticed the faint loom of land abeam, and pointed it out to the captain, who said 'All right, my boy'. The uneasy mate adjourned to his cabin, climbed fully clothed into his bunk, and left the door ajar to get the drift of what was happening on deck. By this time the wind had veered to WSW and risen to gale force 8, as the sturdy vessel battled valiantly through the heaving billows and monstrous swell. She was proving her worth in these outrageous conditions, and would, no doubt, have carried them all to a safe haven, had not human error intervened. About an hour after going below, the restless mate heard Robert Hancock, the starboard look-out man, give warning of two ships on the lee bow, reaching off, without lights. From this moment disaster was probable, for an Admiralty Inquiry later established that the *Devon* was not on the course stated, which would have kept them well clear of trouble, and that the reported 'Two sail standing out' was almost certainly the dreaded Brison rocks. This would account for subsequent happenings, for if the master believed himself to be on the course the naval investigators reconstructed on their charts, far removed from the dangers of shoal waters and the Brisons, he bore up to pass under their sterns in order to minimise the dangers of collision. The investigators came to the conclusion that, by a sad irony, the series of misadventures

The wreck of the Admiralty cutter

now about to befall the crew would not have happened, had the look-outs been less vigilant.

The mate leapt from his bunk when he heard the excitement on deck, and reached the top of the ladder as both look-outs, now on the port bow, were screaming out 'Rocks! Rocks! Breakers!' 'That's the Brisons, sir,' yelled the horrified mate, as the captain, who was standing on the combings of the main hatch on the port side, summoned all hands to get sail on, in a frantic attempt to gain sufficient way to tack the vessel clear. 'Gather aft the jib sheet! Up peak of mainsail!' he cried. But as they were struggling to carry out these orders, the jib sheet carried away. From this moment calamity was almost inevitable. The captain barked out a series of commands and counter-commands, in a last desperate bid to avert disaster; for, after trying to tack out of a tight situation, he gave orders to clear anchors and let out the best bower anchor. Then, realising that no anchor could possibly be effective in such an overpowering situation, he reverted to his original strategy, urging his men to set more sail. The plucky ship was just beginning to respond, when catastrophe struck. She was dashed against the rocks with such force that she lurched into the air and came to rest broadside-on to the fearful rocks, heavily battered and listing to starboard. Swift attempts to lower the longboat failed as a large sea swept across the vessel and broke it up; brave efforts to lower the dinghy from the stern davits were similarly thwarted as her starboard tackle gave way and she swamped.

It is at moments like this that humanity reveals its true nature. The courageous captain, only too well aware of his own mortality, was acutely conscious of his responsibility towards others in this crisis. As the threatening waters rose and towered and fell and broke and cascaded all about them, and the timbers heaved and crunched and split and fell apart beneath them, he steadied himself on the sloping deck and declared in a clear, firm voice, 'Men, I cannot do anything more for you,' and remained standing in silent prayer. This moved the ship's boy to fall to his knees beside him, and declare his trust in the Lord. Many of the crew seemed mesmerised, clutching onto the superstructure for dear life; others stripped off their heavy garments and dived overboard, in a bid to reach the rocks. The mate hurriedly hacked away his long sea-boots with a sharp knife and, ripping off his jacket and trousers, leapt overboard on the seaward side of the vessel, just as there came a mighty crash and she disappeared beneath the waves for ever. Having sought to avoid the seething waters between the vessel and the rocks, and managed to escape the powerful suction as the ship went down, Davis found himself struggling in the maelstrom with his legs entangled in his drawers, but fortunately he was able to grasp some floating wreckage and free himself from this particular hazard.

He took a heavy battering in these deadly waters, strewn with rocks and debris and pounded by the relentless breakers. But, as fate would have it, the sea yielded him up. He was flung into a tight cleft on the smaller Brison, where he remained in a dazed state throughout that night. Seafarers must have been an extraordinarily tough breed in those days. After having undergone such punishing experiences, to have survived that chill October night, naked, hungry, dehydrated, and exposed, on an inhospitable islet, beset by waves and drenched with spray, seems almost beyond belief. And, as he well knew, his troubles would be far from over even if he made it through 'till morning. For who would be aware of his pathetic plight as a prisoner of the Brisons? Was it his imagination, or did he hear the mournful cries of his despairing shipmates above the tumult of the storm? And could it have been his fancy that those heart-rending cries had died away as the grand and awesome Cornish coastline was stealthily revealing itself in the cold and silvery light of dawn, and that his shipmates had been released from the dangers of wind and wave for ever? In truth, the sea had claimed 17 lives on that fateful night, and all but he had perished.

In the early light of morning, watchers on the shore witnessed the distressing sight of wreckage strewn along the desolate coastline, and knew that the formidable Atlantic had claimed yet another vessel. Keen and practised eyes surveyed the stricken scene of shipwreck, and saw no signs of hope. But one old coastguard, hero of a hundred stormy vigils, instinctively felt there to be a soul in need of human help. Although this optimistic view was discounted by many among the growing congregation of sightseers now lining the cliffs, his insistence that he 'saw a spot of something' heaving with the swell upon the Little Brison, eventually led to the lifeboat being summoned. The ideals of preserving life from shipwreck were such, in this tough, isolated seafaring community, that the indefatigable coxswain, Matthew Nicholas, and his staunch crew preferred the rigours and dangers of launching their lifeboat into the most daunting of conditions, rather than risk the possibility of leaving some poor soul in distress at sea.

Thus it was that the Sennen Cove lifeboat *Cousins William & Mary Ann of Bideford*, crewed by weather-beaten, sinewy fishermen, was launched within 15 minutes of the news reaching them, and they battled through terrific seas with the wind dead against them. It took three hours of very strenuous pulling and contending with being tossed about on the crest of the waves and catapulted into the deep troughs, to get within striking distance of the rocks, where a heavy pall of mist and spray and the mighty roar of the thundering waves made it very difficult to detect possible survivors, or discern cries for help. Nevertheless, they rowed and rowed around the jagged reefs, shouting for all they were worth, until at last they reluctantly decided that it was a wasted mission and they must head for home. But, as Providence would have it, they paused on their oars to take a last, wistful look back at the very moment the weary castaway chose to seek out a more comfortable situation. They spotted each other simultaneously; and what a mighty cheer rang out above the tumult of the waters! In that moment of elation, George Davis, realising that the lifeboat could never get to him, was on the point of diving into the seething waters, and swimming out to them. However, he was directed not to do so by Mr Sylvester Morrison, Chief Coastguard Officer at Sennen, who was aboard the lifeboat with his rocket apparatus. But what a challenge shooting an accurate line would be! Practising on terra firma was one thing; trying to achieve success from the limited confines of a bouncing boat on a rough sea in a gale was quite another, and the kick-back of flame as the rocket was fired would place them all in jeopardy.

Having taken the lifeboat to the leeward of the rocks in order to prepare the apparatus, the crew were dismayed to discover that the stand of the rocket tube was too high. However, these seasoned men of the sea, well used to using their wits in their daily dicing with the ocean, made improvisations, and swiftly lashed the apparatus fore and aft, establishing a line through a ring bolt to allow the trigger to be activated. Thus, Sylvester Morrison, despite the odds placed against him, was able to distinguish himself by shooting an accurate line to the victim on the rock at the first attempt. Then a lifebuoy was fixed to the line and Davis was instructed to haul it in and secure himself into the cork harness. Although weakened by his bizarre experiences and slowed in his normal reactions, his seafaring instincts allowed him to gravitate towards the safest point from which to jump. He stepped into the cork buoy, leapt clear of the sharp rocks, and was deftly hauled in to the safety of the lifeboat by his rescuers, who laid him in the bottom of the boat, covered him over as best they could and headed back to Sennen Cove.

After being landed, he was cared for by the fisherfolk in one of the cottages, and soon recovered from his frightful experiences. And everyone marvelled at the curious coincidence whereby this lifeboat, which had been financed by a Mrs Davis in memory of her husband George, had saved the life of a shipwrecked stranger of the same name. Coxswain Matthew Nicholas and Mr Sylvester Morrison were awarded Silver Medals of the RNLI for this outstanding service.

2

Jack and the *Jean Charcot*

◆

Of all the lifeboat stations scattered around the shores of France, those on the formidable north-west Atlantic coast and off-shore islands have always been of particular importance, and these lifeboatmen enjoy the same kind of prestige and affection that is enjoyed by their Cornish counterparts. So there was great excitement back in May 1939, when a splendid new 42 ft lifeboat, with two 40 hp diesel engines, capable of a speed of 8 knots, arrived on station at Ile Molène, Finistère. They decided to name the sleek, handsome lifeboat after the French explorer, *Jean Charcot*, and looked forward to the prestigious naming ceremony. She was certainly destined to fulfil the promise of her intrepid name, but, in the event, it was many years before that stylish ceremony actually took place, after an initiation by birth, war, the RNLI and Reserve Mechanic Jack Snell . . .

Few lifeboats could claim the distinction of births having taken place aboard them, but then the *Jean Charcot* turned out to be no ordinary lifeboat. This event occurred soon after she came on station in 1939, when Mme Ernest Roger was being taken from one of the islands to a mainland clinic, and the name 'Charcot' was incorporated in the baby's baptismal names. Young Francis was to return this compliment in due course . . .

The next strange occurrence, desperate and dramatic, was recorded in the *Life-Boat War Bulletin No. 3* somewhat mundanely, thus:

'FRENCH AND BELGIAN LIFE-BOATS IN THE BRITISH FLEET
A French life-boat, which escaped from France at the end of June 1940 and arrived at an English port, with her coxswain, motor mechanic and French refugees on board, has been taken over by the Institution for the war. She is now serving in its reserve fleet. A Belgian life-boat, which was picked up derelict in the English Channel by one of H.M. ships has been put at the disposal of the Institution by the Belgian government, free of charge, until the end of the war. The Institution is repairing her, and she too will serve in the reserve fleet.'

Fifty-four years on, I asked my old pal 'Young Janner' Snell, who was born into the elite seafaring and lifeboat fraternity of the Falmouth waterfront, to tell me about his life and times, and this French connection. 'I've never earnt a penny on the land!' he declared proudly, as he settled back comfortably in his favourite fireside chair in his home overlooking the Carrick Roads. 'Always on the water. As a young lad I was always in the boats with my father, "Janner" Snell, who was a lifeboatman for 43 years, and the coxswain of the Falmouth lifeboat for 17 years.

'I went to serve my apprenticeship as a motor and marine engineer in Taylors, in Falmouth, until I was 21. Then I joined the Merchant Navy as an engineer for the Moore Line. After that I was with the New Zealand Shippin' Company, and I was to and fro to Australia then, takin' out cargo and bringin' back frozen meat and fruit.'

Those happy years as an engineer aboard the merchant ships provided him with good technical and other experience, but, having been brought up in a lifeboat family, his real ambition was to be an engineer in the lifeboat. 'So I applied to the Institution in Grosvenor 'Ouse, in London, and was accepted straight away. Then I was sent to Southampton to gain experience with the new lifeboat diesel engines. I was there a fortnight, before I went on the coast, on relief duty.' If there was still a touch of the seafaring rover about him, this and his life-long ambition were to be harnessed and fulfilled in a very agreeable way. 'I joined the Lifeboat Institution, followin' in my father's foot-steps, in June 1939, as a reserve mechanic. The first place I started off was at Salcombe. Then I went to Fowey and Falmouth, the Isles of Scilly and various other stations around the coast. We were roughly three months in each port.

'War was declared on 3rd September 1939, and I was in Fowey at the time. I was over there relievin'. And we were all very upset about it. Everybody was. It was just a matter of what we were goin' to do, and 'ow we were goin' to manage. We were all waitin' for the Germans to come next day, kind of thing. It wasn't as bad as all that until the first bombs started to drop, and then when they did, the cities was terrible. Falmouth was bombed, and my 'ome 'ere, Cromwell Cottage, was damaged from the shock of a bomb dropped at the railway archway near the docks. I was sent to Falmouth, to over'aul the engines of a French lifeboat which 'ad been brought 'ere to Falmouth, in the Little Falmouth Yacht Yard.'

The lifeboat service was 115 years old when the Second World War broke out. The previous year had been the busiest in the Institution's history, and the RNLI was well aware that they would lose valuable lifeboatmen to the Services, and that boatbuilding yards and engineering shops would be requisitioned, at a time when demands on their expertise were likely to increase. Furthermore, a variety of wartime perils, such as mines, blacked-out coasts and diminished navigational aids would be added to the usual hazards of the sea. Experience gained and lessons learnt in the First World War were still fairly fresh in their minds, although technology had moved on considerably since then. At that time seven-eighths of the lifeboat fleet had been sailing boats, with only 19 being motor driven. In the Second World War a much higher percentage of motor-lifeboats, and only 15 sailing lifeboats, were operating around the coasts of the British Isles. Now there was the formidable and increasing hazard of being attacked from the air. All this, with the added possibility of lifeboatmen being overwhelmed by spies or armed casualties being picked up from the seas, brought about the bizarre situation of lifeboatmen, those saviours of life and symbols of mercy and humanity, being armed with guns!

'The most excitin' thing that ever 'appened to me 'appened when the Germans were goin' into France. The lifeboatmen, crew of the island of Molène in the Bay of Biscay, put to sea with refugees in their lifeboat, and ended up at St Mary's on the Isles of Scilly. She was called the *Jean Charcot*. And de Gaulle was in this country, and 'e loaned the Institution the lifeboat until the war was over. I 'ad the honour of over'aulin' the engines of this boat at the Little Falmouth Yacht Yard, and we done a lot of alterations. She was painted green, with a white bottom, and naturally she was repainted in the Institution's colours, which was red, white and blue, and became ON 844. I 'ad the French mechanic with me when we brought the boat over 'ere. While we were workin' on 'er, we were bombed 'ere in Falmouth, and the electrician 'oo 'ad been doin' the electrical work on 'er was killed down at the Wayside Café on the Moor in Falmouth. Called Tommy Pratt.

'When the boat was completed, we went on trials. Then I took 'er on reserve duty all round the coast. The French mechanic was offered a job with the *Jean Charcot*, but 'e and the coxswain joined the Free French over 'ere, and worked for General de Gaulle in French boats. Of course, we were used to the French because we 'ad a lot of French people workin' with us. All the fisherman 'oo used to come 'ere, all worked for the French. Then, the Dutch and the French and we, were what you might say, a mixed navy! We were all different kinds o' people, but all in the same cause.

'At that time each lifeboat was fitted with two rifles. We were all supplied with rifles. They were very old fashioned, and they were Canadian rifles. Just in case you picked up a German airman 'oo was 'imself armed, 'oo could take charge o' the boat. I 'ad to take a gunnery course down to the docks. If I didn't take this course they would've sent soldiers in the lifeboat with me when I went on passage. So, to avoid that I took this course to gain experience on a strip Lewis gun, before they'd allow me to go out with a machine gun aboard. 'Ad to go down to the docks to 'ave this thing fitted in the boat to use if we wanted. For we was goin' to pick up a convoy off Land's End. Seein' we were goin' on passage from one place to another, we used to go in convoy, if this was necessary. And they thought this was a good idea. Falmouth was an assembly place for convoys. You were there in case the convoy was attacked, and you could do some good. And in any case you 'ad a safe passage to your next port. And we were goin' up to Fishguard, in South Wales. I couldn't go unless I took two soldiers aboard. Or if I was willin' to take a course, they would eliminate the soldiers. We could go on our own then. So long as you 'ad somebody aboard 'oo could use the gun. But some of the reserve lifeboats 'ad to take two soldiers with them. I 'ad to take this strip Lewis gun, and when I got to Fishguard, I 'ad to return this to the Admiralty. Wasn't allowed to keep the gun. That was very interestin', very interestin'.' I asked Jack if there was ever a time that the guns aboard his lifeboat ever had to be used in earnest. 'No. Never fired on, or under attack.'

The situation of war meant that harbour lights had to be extinguished all along the coast, together with most of the lighthouses and lightships. Navigational lights on shipping could only be used when there might be a danger of collision, and even then they had to be dimmed. Ships in distress were permitted to burn flares, but lifeboats had to be launched in darkness with the occasional use of short-range flashing lamps and torches. Searchlights could be used to locate a wreck, and in such circumstances, the lifeboat might call for the harbour lights to guide them in. For lifeboatmen, traditionally an independent breed with an intimate knowledge of local waters, the darkness of war was accompanied by the silence of war. The maroons could no longer be fired in an emergency, and there was the unaccustomed discipline of being under the control of the Navy, which meant that no lifeboat could be launched without the permission of the naval officer in charge. In areas scattered with mines, minesweepers had to clear safe channels and safety procedures had to be followed.

'Durin' the war there was no maroons fired, because you' be tellin' where you were. And no radios to be used at all; although I did on one occasion.' Jack chuckled, but kept the secret to himself. 'Yes, you wasn't allowed to use maroons. So I 'ad to be stationed somewhere where the crew could call me within a few minutes of the lifeboat bein' wanted. You 'ad to say exactly where you were, every part of the day. I spent eight or ten years never goin' free of the station, in wartime and afterwards. Just married to it. But I loved the job, and that's part of it.

Jack Snell and 'Jean Charcot'

But if I went to the pictures, I 'ad to tell the usherette in the cinema where I was sittin', in case I was wanted. If a 'plane came down or anythin'.

'Bein' a diesel boat, the *Jean Charcot*, we 'ad to be towed in and out of Falmouth by a steam tug, three miles out to sea, in case we set off the mines in the bay. In the early part of the war a mine went off and sunk a ship. She was the *Caroni River*, an American T2 tanker. They was out in the bay doin' trials, and she went up with a mine. There was a lot of mines dropped down 'ere in the bay. I expect there's a few out there now. We 'ad to be towed out by a steamer, 'cos the diesel engine I 'ad were thumpin'. That was very interestin'. I won't say it was essential, but 'twas like everythin' else, you've got to be careful and take precautions. You've got to be thorough. And before we left port, it 'ad to be through the Admiralty, and I'd be several days waitin' to see when we could go. If we were goin' from one place to another, then we ran in convoy. I've been in several convoys in the Irish Sea. Then when you're goin' to leave, you gotta tell them that you're leavin', and to what port you're goin'. The Admiralty 'ere in Falmouth took over several rooms in 'otels out on the seafront and other places. We couldn't go anywhere we wanted to go. We 'ad to go where the Institution sent us. They used to send me Sailin' Orders.

'I was based anywhere, where the lifeboat was relievin' the station boat. And that would be at Fowey and Falmouth, Padstow, Appledore, Fishguard and the 'ole of Wales. That's all the stations in Wales and right up to 'Oly'ead. Fishguard, Beaumaris, Menai Straits, and then up to St Annes. And all the way back round the coast again. Then, after the war, in other boats, right up to Tor Bay, Brixham, Wells and Cromer. The crew would always find me accommodation wherever I went. This lifeboat, this *Jean Charcot,* was well known on the Welsh coast. Everybody knew 'er, bein' French, and the name . . . I was with 'er five years . . . She was a beautiful boat. I wish I could 'ave married 'er! But 'course she wasn't so good as the Institution's boats, naturally. Not built under the same style. She was more or less like a Watson type. But she'd 'ave galvanised nails, instead o' brass screws. Put it that way. But beautiful built. Strong. Beautiful built. At Beaumaris Yacht Yard, she was refastened underneath with brass screws. That cost a penny! Morris and Levet was the boatbuilders. She went in there two or three times for over'aulin'.

'I know another lifeboat, too, was picked up in the Channel. A lifeboat from Belgium. Well, another reserve engineer like myself, called Billy Mann, 'e was put in charge of 'er. Funny thing, we joined the Institution on the same day! And another funny thing, 'e was on relief duty in this country as well. And we come alongside each other, up at

'Oly'ead, one day. Two foreign boats. 'Twas up on the wharf at 'Oly'ead. 'E'd been over to Douglas on relief duty, and 'e came across on passage, comin' home down to 'Oly'ead. And I 'appened to be there with the *Jean Charcot*. We were alongside each other. An amazin' thing. To think that two boats that more or less run away from 'ome . . . And one was picked up in the Channel. We don't know why or 'ow. But she was.

'I enjoyed the Institution's way of workin', as a mechanic in my own lifeboat. I was always a mechanic in my own boat. Their crew would come aboard o' me when their boat was 'avin' an over'aul. But I would still be in charge of the machinery, and was always in charge of the boat. Me and the *Jean Charcot*, we never left each other! Then their crew would come aboard, and whatever duties they 'ad on board their own boat, they would be the same on mine. I enjoyed it all, and around the different stations. It's not like just bein' in one place, when you're talkin' to people. You can talk to people wherever you go. So it's a lovely experience. A complete experience. I met some fantastic people. At Beaumaris and the Menai Straits they used to say, "Hallo, John, bach; how long you 'ome for?"

'Only went to one disaster, when we picked up an airman's leg and boots. That was in 1944, in Porthdinllaen, in North Wales. And we see the tail of this 'plane comin' off. She 'ad 'er rudder shot off, and nose-dived into the bay. And, well, there was an 'ell of a stink at the time. We went away. Fortunately, we found where the 'plane sank, 'cos there's a buoy comes up from the 'plane, to tell you. So they can tell where the 'plane goes down. And all we done was pick up the body. 'Is leg was shot off, and we found 'is leg in the boot. 'Twas a terrible thing. We came back to Porthdinllaen and turned 'im over to the Navy's Air Sea Rescue. And I remember there was part of a letter comin' out of 'is pocket. 'Twas from 'is mother, sayin' "Good landin's, Son" 'Twas a terrible thing.

'It's amazin', you know. We went out to these airmen, but the positions were not always correct. We'd be out there, maybe all night, lookin'. And we finally got inshore and discovered it was miles from where you'd been lookin'. Sometimes about 40 miles. There'd be the Admiralty and the coastguards . . . You've gotta 'ave somebody to blame, 'aven't you? Poor devils, they 'ad a 'ard time, too. But we were in very good 'ands with the coastguards and suchlike. They were wonderful people.'

The spirit of the lifeboatmen and the camaraderie of those times, when the population was united in a common cause, combined to make the RNLI a particularly special institution in those dark days of war. 'The spirit of the RNLI was fantastic. I think we done the job because we loved it. And it was an achievement to do somethin' to 'elp people. Oh, yes. Because, you see, everyone . . . doesn't matter 'oo you were; doesn't matter whether you were in the lifeboats, the Services or ashore, you were all in it. And we did pull together. And one certain thing; you just lived for today. And I think we were 'appier than what we are now.

'In bad weather, you always regard your boat as a 'uman bein', as a part of you. And when you come into port after experiencin' a very bad day, you kind o' say, "Well, we've made it, old girl, we're in port and we've made it together." It's just somethin' that a boat becomes a part of you. And I think anyone 'oose connected with the sea and boats would realise exactly what I'm sayin', and 'ave exactly the same feelin's. And I always look up on the One Above, 'oo 'as allowed us to 'andle the sea, as the sea is master, always. And if we are allowed to ride on it with the 'elp of the One Above, that is a great goodness.

'The *Jean Charcot*, she was a lovely boat, and she done a lot of services throughout all the stations she'd been with. Very reliable. When the war was over, I took 'er back from Fleetwood to Newlyn, to turn 'er over, back to the French. And they 'oisted the flag; put a French flag up, which my crew didn't enjoy! And they walked ashore! Nearly broke my 'eart when I 'ad to give 'er over. But they were amazed to see what she looked like, bein' under the Institution colours and reconditioned, with several things on deck, which they didn't 'ave and we put there. They were amazed to see 'er. Because she 'ad sails when she came 'ere. But we done away with all that. But we 'ad to take the sails and the mast, all this gear, and give them what she came with. She was a beautiful boat. She was 42 ft long, and a lovely sea boat. But of course, today, with the modern lifeboats, she would be absolutely obsolete now. It's all speed now. It's all 18 knots . . . But we were averagin' 8 knots, and that was a good speed.

'She left Newlyn to go back to the island of Molène, towing two French fishin' boats 'oo were out of action. Couldn't get the parts for their engines. I never 'eard no more about 'er. I'd love to know what 'appened to 'er. She was a lovely boat. She was a part of me. After five years, it is a part of you . . .'

Could those who compiled these reports documenting the return of the French lifeboat, in Britain and France, ever have dreamt about Reserve Mechanic Jack Snell's relationship with the *Jean Charcot*, and their unique place in modern maritime history?

Life-Boat War Bulletin No. 21, September 1945:

'FRENCH LIFE-BOAT RETURNS

In April, less than a month before the war ended, a French life-boat which had served on the British coast for nearly four years, was returned to the French Service. She was the *Jean Charcot* of Isle Molène, on the coast of Brittany. In June 1940 she had escaped from France, with her coxswain, motor mechanic and refugees on board, and came to England. The Ministry of Shipping handed her over to the Institution, which put her in its reserve fleet. She served at eleven different stations in Devon, Cornwall, Wales and Lancashire.'

'SOCIÉTÉ NATIONALE DE SAUVETAGE EN MER
LES STATIONS DE SAUVETAGE
des abords de Brest

(Appendix No. 1, 1946)
Celui de Molène, le *Jean-Charcot*, avait gagné l'Angleterre en juin 1940. Grâce aux bons soins de la Royal National Life-Boat Institution, qui l'a utilisé comme canot de réserve dans ses stations, il nous a été rendu en très bon état.'
(The *Jean Charcot* lifeboat of Molène, arrived in the United Kingdom in June, 1940. She was carefully looked after by the Royal National Lifeboat Institution, who used her as a reserve lifeboat, and returned her to us in a very good state.)

As it transpired, the christening ceremony of the *Jean Charcot* took place eleven years after she had originally arrived on station at Molène, and she had accomplished a number of fine rescues with her coxswain, Charles Masson, and his crew since returning from foreign parts. The ceremony was conducted by His Excellency Monseigneur Fauvel of Quimper, and eleven year old Francis Roger, who had been born aboard her just before she fled on her errand of mercy, was chosen to be her godfather. It was a touching moment as a bottle of wine was broken over her graceful bow, and her stylish escort vessel *Grenadier* fired a traditional salute.

Unfortunately, this charming story did not have the happy ending it deserved. For on the 4th September 1956, tragedy struck as the *Jean Charcot* was launching to the aid of the yacht *Mathan*, which had gone aground on the island of Béniguet. As the lifeboat, aboard her trolley, was travelling down the slipway at speed, the progress of the trolley was halted, and the lifeboat shot forwards and capsized on the beach. Charles Masson, who had been standing at the wheel, got trapped beneath the boat, and sustained a broken spine, and Olivier Masson, who was similarly trapped, had to have his leg amputated. Louis Cariou, who was found in the engine-house, had to be cut free, and was unfit for work for two months, while Maxime le Bousse and Louis Masson were badly bruised. As for the dear old *Jean Charcot*, who had performed a proud humanitarian role in times of war and peace, she had to be condemned. She was replaced by a new lifeboat, which took over her prestigious name.

But:

Her ghost lingers on
In those seas she knew well,
With her roving mechanic
Called 'Young Janner' Snell.

3

The Sunken Land of Lyonesse

◆

'Between Land's End and Scilly rocks
Sunk lies a town that ocean mocks . . .'

So goes the old adage, reminding us that about a third of the ancient Celtic lands west of the Tamar have been claimed by Neptune, and that tracts which cannot be walked over can be sailed over. For they say that the Isles of Scilly were once united to the coast of mainland Britain, until a flood and tempest of biblical proportions claimed an area of Lethowsow, which came to be known as the lost land of Lyonesse. And therein hangs a tale, beloved by poets and dreamers, and not altogether discounted by geologists.

Centuries ago St Michael's Mount, which rises so majestically from the windswept waters of Mount's Bay today, was situated in the heart of the forest of Guffaer, adjoining the green and fertile lands of Lethowsow. The inhabitants of this mild and salt-sprayed region, who gleaned a humble livelihood from the harvests of the land and of the sea, grew more prosperous as sailing vessels from the ancient ports of the Mediterranean came here to trade in tin. As the years went by, the small, scattered settlements became dominated by one, which assumed the importance of a miniature city. Could it be that those inhabitants developed a taste for wealth, riches and materialistic values, which so often lead to decadence?

Perhaps it was timely when, a few centuries later, a succession of Christian missionaries began to reach these shores from Celtic lands across the seas, borne, some said, on heavy millstones, made buoyant by their faith. Legend suggests that those early saints, erudite and earnest, preached their message of love and hope so well that they inspired their flock to build 140 churches to the glory of God. Those who dwelt in the surrounding countryside were delighted, no doubt, when those multitudinous, melodious bells re-echoed across the land

The Lost Land of Lyonesse

and sea on the Sabbath, while lesser parish churches rang out in humbler tones. Captains of the ships, who used the noble spires for navigational guidance, pulled on the halyards and saluted the fair land of Lyonesse. Did Neptune hear these haunting strains and yearn for the glory that was Lyonesse? Or did he claim this beautiful land to create a turbulent strait and lure more mariners to their doom?

The losing of Lyonesse was a long drawn-out process, hastened at various times by destructive storms of great intensity. Some say that Neptune laid claim to Lyonesse when King Arthur's traitors fled here, when the sea rose mightily and swallowed them up. Be that as it may, the enormous encroachment of the sea, which swamped the land, and turned a lake-in-a-forest into a lake-in-the-sea, came in autumn, when fully-formed hazel nuts hung expectantly on the bough for the harvest which never came. For the submarine forest, revealed at exceptionally low tides around Mount's Bay, and the deep anchorage of Gwavas Lake hold the clues to some of the mysteries, helping to align dreams with reality.

The 11th century had been a particularly bad time for the hardy, seafaring folk who dwelt along these shores, for it started with a violent storm from the Atlantic which flooded the area around St Michael's Mount and drowned many people. In 1014 the *Saxon Chronicle* recorded: 'This year, on St Michael's Mass Eve, came that mickle sea flood widely through this land; and it run up so far as never at no time before; and it drowned many towns, and mankind too innumerable to be computed'. The unsettled pattern continued intermittently throughout the following decades. But if the century had started with a chilling, watery shudder, it went out with a diabolical bang. The sudden inundation which eventually overtook this fabled tract of land between Land's End and the Isles of Scilly probably occurred with the lunar-prima, on the eleventh day of November, in 1099, when the *Saxon Chronicle* returned to its earlier theme, saying: 'This year eke sprang up so much the seaflood and so mickle harm did as no man minded that it ever before did'. This time, not content with clutching the fair land of Lyonesse permanently to his saline bosom, notorious Neptune also stole the Goodwin Sands from the fertile Garden of England, thus creating another maritime trap for vulnerable seafarers in the busy and narrowing confines of the English Channel.

It must have seemed as though the end of the world had come as the lurid skies darkened, the storm winds strengthened and the gathering fury of the wild Atlantic unleashed itself on the frontier cliffs. And for many it had. Frantic cries and screams of desperate humanity were of little significance in the course of this elemental tournament of wind and wave and rock; a tournament won by the sea, as the weakened rocks suddenly exploded and the ferocious Atlantic roared and gushed over this fertile tract of land, claiming the sheep, the cattle, the sophisticated city and all who dwelt therein.

Well, perhaps not all, for according to legend the fearless warrior Trevelyan, who owned extensive lands around these parts, escaped the perils of the deep in grand, heroic style, emerging from the boiling surf astride a fleet, white charger, and taking refuge in a cave on the Perranuthnoe shores. And, indeed, this Herculean feat was depicted in the family's coat of arms. It was said that a fellow landowner, Lord Goonhilly, who also defied the terrors of the tempest, but possibly with less panache, erected a chapel on the Sennen shores in thanksgiving for his divine deliverance.

Since that time generations of fishermen have dredged up a variety of domestic artefacts, including sections of windows and doors, and chunks of masonry, and ancient foundations have been revealed at low tides around the submerging Isles of Scilly. Sailors regarding the Seven Stones reef as the highest tips of Lyonesse always referred to them as 'The City', and some even claimed to have seen the shapes of rooftops and spires when the ocean was exceptionally calm. Some say that the ghostly sound of a myriad of bells can still be heard re-echoing from Neptune's kingdom.

And who knows for whom the bells will one day toll? For, with ever rising sea levels, your house – or mine – could be pickled in brine!

4

The Mermaid of Zennor

◆

'Here everybody comes to church, up this path lined with stones as old as Roman Britain, for none leaves Zennor without looking for the mermaid. She is on one of the two old bench ends, now part of a little seat in the sanctuary, and we see her with her mirror in one hand and a comb in the other combing her long tresses. She must have been in the church when it was new 500 years ago.'
(*The King's England CORNWALL* by Arthur Mee, 1937)

The village of Zennor was a notoriously rough old place in days of yore, when the rumbustious revels of a Saturday night, after the miners had received their pay, would leave many a miner, labourer or fisherman bleeding in the gutter, nursing a broken head or seeking a remedy for an all-consuming hangover, as the tuneful church bells rang out their pious message of peace and goodwill of a Sunday morning. Those who made it to the church, for the benefit of their souls, often continued to the Tinners' Arms across the road, for more spiritual refreshment, comradeship and the chance to exchange a yarn or two around the fireside in the traditional way. Everyone in the parish, whatever the means by which they earned a meagre crust, had close connections with the sea.

Old Mawgan, who usually occupied a well-appointed bench in a corner of the tavern, was of a philosophical bent, believing that there was more to heaven and earth than fish, feather, fur or man. This amiable and relaxed God-fearing man, who listened so attentively to the parson, was not averse to a bit of poaching and freetrading here and there, nor a pint or two of best ale afterwards. He had been sailing particularly close to the wind on the night he met some strangers who were curious about the carving of a mermaid in the church. So he called for some ale, requested the landlord's daughter to stoke up the peaty log fire, lit up his pipe, cleared his husky throat, looked reflective and began. 'This 'ere is a tale wot was told to me at my mother's knee. An' it was tol' to 'er by 'er mother, 'oo 'eard it from 'er ole granfer, 'oo was

The encounter while at anchor in Pendower Bay

in the church choir when it 'appened. So it 'as ter be true; true as wot I'm sittin' 'ere, feelin' some thirsty, on account of a partic'arly 'ard day's work at sea.' The visitors took the hint, and kept his tankard flowing while he recounted this strange tale.

It seems that when this particular granfer was a lad, there was an old fellow living at the windy ridge, by the name of Christmas. Nobody knew him by any other name, but some hinted that he was a descendant of the ill-fated Pengerswicks, who once dwelt on the southern shores. But despite his holy-sounding name, he had little time for the parson and his dreary sermons, and was more interested in taking a horn of beer than taking Holy Communion. He married late in life, and when a beautiful baby daughter arrived, he popped into the Tinners' Arms to wet the baby's head with some of his old cronies. When they asked him what they were going to call the child, he said 'Marina', for her eyes were of the deepest blue, like the colour of the ocean on a sunshiny day. 'When's the christenin'?' they asked, for they wanted to give her a silver spoon. 'The Devil take you and your silver spoon!' retorted the new father ungraciously. 'There ain't gonna be no christenin!' 'No christenin'?' said one, taken aback at this outburst. 'Why if you don't get 'er christened, she'll never find any rest in this world, or the next.' 'Don't give me no parson's talk', growled old Christmas, downing his pint and preparing to walk out. 'If 'er soul should pass into a merrymaid (mermaid), then she would be doomed to swim the Seven Seas for ever more', said another. 'Don't talk such rubbish. I don't believe that, an' neither do you,' he said, sweeping out of the bar room, slamming the heavy oak door behind him.

The years went by and the pretty child with raven curls and deep blue eyes, grew into a fine young woman. Even so, folk always reckoned that there was something rather strange about her. She tended to prefer her own company, remaining aloof from other people, and she seemed to have a faraway look in those beautiful limpid eyes, particularly when she sat on the cliffs and gazed out to sea, as she so often did. But, despite all this, there was not a lad in the parish who was not in love with her. Most of these love-lorn lads, realising that their situation was hopeless, married lesser beauties, and only thought about her in their dreams. But, if the truth be told, there was one young man she longed for with all her heart, and he was the Squire's son, Mark Trewhella. But the course of true love never did run smoothly, and he had been forbidden to see her by his overbearing father, who said that she was a mere fisherman's daughter, who had never been received into the church.

Christmas adored his only child, and always let her have her own way. He hated to see her pout those pretty lips or furrow her fine brow. Although it was customary for fishermen to keep their women-folk away from fishing and the sea, considering it to be unlucky and preferring them to remain at home and follow the traditions of domesticity and good-wifeliness, Marina had always been allowed to help her father in his boat. She was never happier than when she was on the sea, and then her father noticed that the wistful expression disappeared, giving way to radiance and light and laughter.

One day Marina decided to take a solitary trip in her father's fishing boat without seeking his permission. She was well-versed in the skills of the sea; it was second nature to her, for she had occupied a place in this boat before she had taken her first, faltering steps on land. This being the case, no one could ever understand how it was that she came to topple overboard on a calm day as she drew in the net, and why the sea never yielded her up. Old Christmas and his wife were heart-broken. Not a day went by without they thought about her, and everyone noticed that they suddenly became the most regular attenders at the church. It was a cruel loss, also, for the Squire's son, who bore his grief in silence, and eventually married to fulfil his father's wish to produce a son and heir to carry on the estate.

Many years later, when the rumbustious reputation of Zennor folk had mellowed a little, the village became renowned for the sweet singing of the choirboys in the church, particularly young Matthew Trewhella, whose heavenly voice could be heard wafting across the sea by the fishermen, who reported unusually good catches at such times.

The congregation was often swelled by visitors from neighbouring parishes, who came to hear the delightful singing for themselves. Among the many strangers thus enticed to the church was a striking young woman with compelling blue eyes and long, black hair, who always wore a dark blue cloak and a softly flowing, shimmering sea-green gown which reached to the floor. The whole congregation was captivated by the power and purity of her voice; indeed, young Matthew Trewhella could never take his eyes off her, and it was noticed that she often stole furtive glances at him. Although her divine singing rose above the sound of others in the church, she never spoke to anyone. As soon as the service was over she swept down the aisle, and seemed to glide through the open doorway and disappear over the hills. The strange thing was that no one could ever discover where she came from or where she went.

One Sunday, when the congregation was particularly large, her dark, alluring eyes became fixed on young Matthew, and he appeared like one entranced. As she turned to leave the church, the handsome lad, who bore a particular resemblance to his grandfather, Mark Trewhella, was compelled to follow. Folk knew that they were in love. Some said they made a handsome couple as they left the church together, hand in hand. But, sad to say, they disappeared over the hills and were never seen again. The heart went out of the village choir, and the neighbourhood was all the poorer for their going.

No one would have guessed their fate, had it not been for the captain of a sailing vessel, coming to anchor in Pendower Bay one Sunday morning. He heard a sweet voice hailing his ship, and to his amazement beheld a dark-eyed, raven-haired merrymaid, naked to the waist, arising from the water. She requested him, very politely, to pull up his anchor and hasten away, for he was blocking the entrance to her subterranean home, imprisoning her husband and children inside. 'I've seen that pretty face afore, Cap'n!' cried one of his crewmen. 'Years ago, when I were a lad in the church choir, along wi' poor Matthey Trewhella, wot was never seen again. It's 'aunted me ever since. She'm up to no good, Cap'n, an' my flesh is a-creepin'!'

No ship can ever have weighed anchor and set sail as rapidly as this one, in the crew's determination to escape from this siren of the sea. 'I've aged years since the days we was in the 'ole church choir,' the grey-bearded old sea-dog told his mates in the tavern afterwards, 'but this 'ere merrymaid, 'er looked as young an' beautiful as ever!'

'Time and tide wait for no mortal man,' declared old Mawgan, observing the timepiece on the wall and draining the contents of his tenth tankard. 'Put another log on the fire,' called the landlord to his daughter. 'There's a chill in the air tonight.'

5

The Capricious *Lady Daphne*

◆

Back in July 1984, the waterfront fraternity of Falmouth was intrigued by the unexpected appearance of the handsome Rochester ketch barge *Lady Daphne*, which was escorting and acting as mother ship to some of the Drake Fellowship's restored shrimp boats taking part in the week-long Falmouth Regatta. 'A journey back in time!' declared boatman Jimmy Morrison, who had been aboard her on a courtesy trip at Mylor Yacht Club and had taken a turn at her wheel. 'It's like seein' an ol' friend again, after all these years. The last time I saw 'er was in September 1939, just after the war broke out. It was 'er last trip from Rochester to Falmouth, and I discharged a 'undred ton of cement for 'Arvey's & Co. of Falmouth, and a 'undred ton to 'Arvey's of Truro.'

'She's a fair ol' lady, with quite a past,' chuckled marine artist Tony Warren, as she prepared to sail on down to the Isles of Scilly, scene of some frisky, youthful exploits, having fulfilled a sedate and motherly role in Falmouth. And we yarned away about it on Custom House Quay, in the time honoured style.

The Christmas of 1927 was remembered by one and all around these parts, as being one of the few white Yuletides experienced within living memory. For the usually mild regions of West Devon and Cornwall had caught the tail-end of a spectacular snowstorm, thought to be approaching the severity of the notorious blizzard of March 1891.

All seemed set fair on Christmas morning as the *Lady Daphne*, skippered by Theodore Whitby, assisted by crewman Kenneth Mann and cook Jhansi Green, left Weymouth for the port of Fowey. But a heavy gale sprang up at about two o'clock in the afternoon, and they soon found themselves being buffeted about in a blinding snowstorm. This sudden wind out of hell increased in violence, tore the mainsail to ribbons, then carried the topsail away. In a fearsome battle with the raging elements, it took all three of them to move the ship's wheel, and Captain Whitby, who had weathered many a storm in his day, breathlessly admitted that these were the very worst conditions he had ever encountered, and that the best thing they could do was make for the

Whiteout – the 'Lady Daphne' in distress

haven of Plymouth. But as they fought to manoeuvre the heavy wheel, the ship gave a mighty lurch. The captain was flung overboard, and was swallowed up immediately in the raging seas. The shocked young crewmen, unable to launch the ship's boats in such conditions, hurriedly flung a couple of lifebelts overboard in the vain hope that he might be able to grasp them as the *Lady Daphne* swept past the harbour entrance and careered on madly down the Channel. The brave young mariners did their best to keep cool-headed in this diabolical situation, and attempted to make for the port of Falmouth. But the vessel was out of control, and they hoped that they would be able to round the Lizard and gain the safety of Mount's Bay.

'The weather grew worse, and the cold was so terrible that the water froze on our faces,' said crewman Mann afterwards. 'I could not feel my hands, and all I could do was to try to steer with both my wrists. We burnt flare after flare and sent up distress signals, and once a steamer came up to within three or four lengths of us, but when she saw that we were only a barge, she made off again. When we were about ten miles off the Lizard about 4 am on Monday, we burnt some flares and, with the exception of the steamer I have referred to, we had the first answers to our signals, and they were from the land – I believe it was from the lighthouse, or from Lloyds Signal Station, where two rockets were sent up.

'You can imagine our terrible anxiety, for I thought it was all up with us, and I did not expect to see the land again. After a time the Lizard motor lifeboat came out, and we had to make a jump for it. Green was the first to jump, and he nearly lost his life, for he almost fell into the boiling sea; but the bowman of the lifeboat managed to grasp him in time. I was going to jump when I found it was impossible, and the lifeboat had to come back a second time for me. Eventually I made the jump and got on board safely, and we were taken to the Lizard and landed, and treated with every kindness.

'It was the worst Christmas I have ever spent. I have been with Captain Whitby for three years. He has been more than a father to me, and was one of the straightest men who ever lived.' Both crewmen were cared for at the Royal Cornwall Sailors' Home, in Falmouth.

This may have been where the story ended as far as her crew were concerned, but the *Lady Daphne's* escapade touched other people, and other places. Amongst other things it turned out to be the fitting last service for the distinguished Lizard lifeboat *Frederick H. Pilley*, topping up the number of lives saved to 130, in a feat of great skill and courage. When the *Lady Daphne's* distress signals were first spotted, the lifeboat was swiftly launched and deftly cut an oblique course through the storm-torn waters, to a theoretical point worked out by the radio station. The lifeboatmen were not able to locate the barge at first, but eventually their display of handlights was rewarded by the response of a weak light flickering in the offing. For, just in the nick of time, the two surviving bargemen had managed to ignite some waste with the last few drops of paraffin remaining in their cabin lamp.

The *Lady Daphne* was driving westwards at breakneck speed, and it was not until a point twelve miles WSW of the Lizard that they were able to close with her. It was a manoeuvre fraught with hazards, for both vessels were being flung about violently in the raging seas, with the risk of collision, or lifeboatmen being crushed to death or flung overboard. In the event, with superb skill and perfect timing, anticipating the movements of the wind and waves, they took both men off, and left the battered *Lady Daphne* to her fate.

The Cornishman of 5th January 1928 gives engaging detail of another story within a story thus:

'OLD SOLDIER TAKES SON'S PLACE

When the motor lifeboat at the Lizard was called out during the Christmas holiday, to the help of a ketch which had got completely out of control, one of the regular members of the crew was away. His father, a man of about 60, and an ex-soldier, felt it his duty to take his son's place, although he was a landsman and a heavy gale was blowing. He not only went out but probably saved the bowman's life. While the lifeboat was alongside the ketch, and the bowman was standing by to help one of the crew into the lifeboat, the old soldier saw that the ketch's boom was swinging down on him, and might sweep him overboard, so he promptly knocked him down, much to the bowman's annoyance, until he realised that he had been saved.'

Meanwhile the abandoned *Lady Daphne*, with her sails in tatters and flying a distress signal, was blown in front of the howling easterly gale, with her wheel set to maintain a steady course. Next morning she was sighted by some Scillonians as she drifted with wind and tide towards the Eastern Isles and St Mary's. However, it was assumed that she had a man aboard with local knowledge, as she tacked on through Crow Sound and over Crow Bar in classical style, miraculously avoiding the array of islands, rocks and ledges in her self-steered course. The onlookers, anticipating an equally smart rounding off to anchor, watched in disbelief as she centred on and grounded on the spit of sand off Tresco, and, amazingly, ran ashore without sustaining further damage. The crew of St Mary's lifeboat, who had rushed to her assistance, were astonished to discover that she was 'manned' only by a canary, singing in a cage.

'They lowered all 'er gear – took the mainmast down, tidied 'er up, and with 'er mizzen-mast still in position, she was refloated and towed 'ere to Falmouth for repairs,' concluded Tony. 'Seafarers 'ave long wondered at this strange set of occurrences, for the chances of an abandoned ship adoptin' such expert navigational tactics and comin' to rest relatively unscathed, are very remote. But this 'ere *Lady Daphne*, she seemed to 'ave a mind of 'er own!'

If the capricious *Lady Daphne*'s repertoire of hair-raising capers brought tragedy to some, they brought good luck to others. For shortly afterwards *The Cornishman* reported:

'SCILLONIAN BOATMEN'S GOOD FORTUNE
SALVAGE AWARD OF £580

St Mary's, Scilly, Tuesday
Underwriters visited Scilly and awarded £580 to the Scilly lifeboatmen and trot boat for the salvage of the London ketch *Lady Daphne*, whose captain was washed overboard. The crew were taken off by the Lizard lifeboat about a week ago. The *Lady Daphne* drifted into the roadstead most miraculously. The men will share nearly £40 each.'

6

A Navigational Catastrophe

◆

'These Islands lie to the westward of the 'Lands-End' of 'Cornwall' nine or ten Leagues, and are many Islands and Rocks, you may see them six and seven Leagues off the South West: Part of these Islands are very rocky, but are bold. On the Southermost big Island there standeth an high 'Light-house', erected by the Corporation of the 'Trinity-House' of 'Deptford-Strond', and is a most excellent good Light, and may be seen six or seven Leagues off. Before this 'Light-house' was erected, there was not a Winter but there were some ships cast away: but since the erecting of it, there hath not a Ship been lost, but by Ignorance; so that Navigation is much obliged to the great Care of the 'Trinity-House' in erecting this Light.'
(Directions for Sailing in & out at the Several Sounds at the Islands of Scilly: Great Britain's Coasting Pylot: *1693: Captain Greenvile Collins*)

These words were written a few years before one of the greatest maritime disasters of all time occurred on these treacherous shores. We will never know why the flagship *Association*, which was bound for the Channel, was standing so far towards the north, nor why the look-outs did not observe the warning lights. Confusing and conflicting reports surround the sequence of events which occurred on that fateful twenty-second day of October in 1707, while subsequent happenings gave rise to a variety of interpretations.

Cloudesley Shovel had been a Norfolk lad of humble birth, before running away to sea as a cabin boy and scaling his way up the promotional ladder, with a flair for being credited with noteworthy achievements. He had demonstrated ingenuity and artfulness when it came to sorting out piratical antics, and decisive naval strategy in regard to foreign fleets. In short, he was a hard man, as befitted the hard times in which he served, and he emerged as a Knight and Rear Admiral of all England.

After the capture of Gibraltar and the siege of Toulon, the British 21-vessel fleet, commanded by Sir Cloudesley Shovel aboard the flagship *Association*, was on its way home when it ran into foul weather in the vicinity of the Isles of Scilly. As there was some uncertainty as to the exact position, orders were given to lie-to; soundings were taken and Sir Cloudesley conferred with the captains about what latitude they were in. All agreed that they were off Ushant, on the coast of France, apart from the master of the *Lenox*, who maintained that they must be further north than that, and likely to sight the Isles of Scilly in about three hours or so. Sir Cloudesley, accepting the strong consensus of opinion, and brushing aside this solitary note of caution, signalled for the fleet to resume sailing at six o'clock, by which time a freshening breeze had erupted from the south-south-west.

Tradition says that a sailor lad from Scilly, aboard the flagship, who knew these waters well, warned the officer of the watch that they were heading for disaster, for the light they made for was Scilly light. Whereupon his shipmates laughed and swore at him, saying it was merely a sail and ship's lanthorn on the horizon. This was reported to Sir Cloudesley, who sent for the lad to discipline him for such insubordination, but when he had the effrontery to insist that it *was* so, the great man flew into a rage, and ordered that he be hanged from the yard-arm. However, he did have the grace to grant a last request, that the chaplain should be allowed to read him the 109th Psalm, which contained curses and prophesies of doom, beginning:

'Hold not thy peace, O God of my praise. For the mouth of the wicked and the mouth of the deceitful are opened against me: they have spoken against me with a lying tongue. They compassed me about also with words of hatred; and fought against me without a cause . . . Set thou a wicked man over him: and let Satan stand at his right hand. When he shall be judged, let him be condemned: and let his prayer become sin. Let his days be few; and let another take his office . . .'

These were brutal days, and the apocryphal story goes that as soon as the sailor's body was committed to the deep, the tempest broke, and the horrified shipmates beheld the gruesome spectacle of the corpse breaking free from the improvised shroud to twist and toss and turn in the troubled wake of the ship. Some say that many of them knew they were doomed before catastrophe struck, but perhaps this horrifying anecdote was added or distorted in the passing of the years, with the telling and re-telling of the tale.

The homeward ships, guided by the *Association*, steered a course east-by-north in thick and dirty conditions, confidently supposing that they had the wide Channel before them. But, in the blackness of that inauspicious night, those aboard the leading vessel suddenly became

The 'Association' striking the rocks

aware that they were surrounded by rocks, and must have realised that their destruction was imminent. In a scene of pandemonium and terror the men of the doomed *Association* fired three guns to warn the following ships of the danger. But it was too late for them and the other leading ships, who were already in the clutches of the notorious Western Reef. The *Association* struck the Gilstone Rock with such tremendous force that she broke up in minutes. She was followed, in quick succession, by the *Eagle* and the *Romney*. The fireship *Firebrand* also foundered upon the rocks, but some of her crew escaped in a boat. The *Phoenix*, which was being driven towards the shore, was abandoned by Captain Sansom and his crew. By a strange quirk of fate, the massive wave, which had played its part in dealing a fatal blow to the *Association* was the means of deliverance for the *St George*, carrying it out of the danger zone. Thanks to the foreboding booms of gunfire, Sir George Byng, a mile to windward aboard the *Royal Anne*, was able to save his vessel, although she was said to have had such a close encounter with the Trenemer Rock that her quarter gallery was carried away. The following fleet was similarly able to take evasive action. But the sorrowful irony of it all was that, having survived swashbuckling sea battles and deadly skirmishes, 1,800 brave young lives were lost on the homeward voyage, as the result of this catastrophic navigational error.

To begin with it was said that only one man had survived from the first three battleships wrecked on the Gilstone, and that he was washed up on the reef known as Hellweathers, where he remained for some days before being rescued. He was subsequently named as George Laurence, quartermaster aboard the *Romney*. This badly injured victim of shipwreck was tended by a local gentleman and a physician from one of the vessels in port. As for the fate of Sir Cloudesley Shovel, posterity will never be absolutely certain of the true sequence of events. Initially it seemed that his body was washed up on the Scilly shore, discovered by local folk, identified by documents found about his person, and given a decent burial in the sands of Porth Hellick Bay. There were conflicting reports as to who actually found the body, but the common factor was that it was devoid of the precious rings which Sir Cloudesley had long worn, which had made deep indentations in his fingers. His heart-broken wife, who had also lost two sons by a previous marriage in the disaster, did all she could to recover these priceless mementoes, in particular the emerald ring which had been the gift of her husband's intimate friend James, Lord Dursley, but nobody seemed to know anything about them. There were gruesome accounts of his body being dug up for further investigation, and it was transported to London for burial in Westminster Abbey.

Many years later, after the death of Lady Shovel, a local woman made a terrible confession to a clergyman on her deathbed. The tortured soul revealed that the admiral was weak, but still alive, when he was cast up on the shore, and that she had murdered him for the sake of his rings and his clothes. She had been afraid to sell the emerald ring for fear of being found guilty of such a cruel and heartless crime, and handed it over to the parson, saying that she could not die in peace until she had made this confession. So the ring was returned to Lord Dursley, who had been aboard the *St George*, and had been spared the cruel fate of countless friends and fellow mariners, on one of the blackest days of maritime history.

7

The Allure of Dollar Cove

Whether the warm sun sparkles on a calm, blue sea, or whether storm winds rage, a faint or fearful aura of foreboding hangs over the magnificent wild and windswept shores of the Lizard peninsula, where countless ships and sailors met a cruel fate. But if almost every rock and cove could tell a pitiful tale of storm and shipwreck, the rugged, wave-pounded shores of Gunwalloe could also boast of sunken treasures and the riches of kings; wealth far beyond the dreams of avarice. For, over the centuries, a spectacular series of shipwrecks yielded up their precious cargoes on this perilous strand, whereupon the lawless population rushed to the shores, and some grew rich on the proceeds. But the wreck which gave rise to the colloquially named Dollar Cove, and continues to excite treasure seekers to this very day, occurred in the 1780s.

Some say that this vessel from the Spanish Main, heavily laden with a cargo of silver specie (coin), was driven ashore one stormy night, having failed to round the Lizard Point. Others maintain that she was trying to escape from Algerine pirates when she encountered fog, and became embayed. Be that as it may, she apparently struck a ridge of rocks beneath the cliffs of Halzephron, heeled over and spilt her precious cargo of silver coins into a narrow, rocky gully as she broke up. In this turbulent area of ever-shifting sands, the forces of nature conspired to bury the bulk of the treasure and retain the secret of its whereabouts. It is said that the natural formation of this little cove resembles a horseshoe; but will it ever bring good luck to the treasure seekers?

Excited local folk who flocked to the scene in the time-honoured way were frequently rewarded with a dollar or two, and cheeky lads from the neighbouring farms who arrived here at croust (lunch) time, swinging their buckets, often returned home with satisfied smirks on their faces. By the end of that century, quite a substantial number of coins had been discovered. But if 19 tons of silver had indeed been spontaneously jettisoned as the vessel broke up, this was merely a drop in the ocean. As the years went by and hundreds of people became caught up in the excitement of the Gold Rush overseas, others preferred to try their luck in securing the silver treasure which lurked beneath the shifting sands of Cornwall.

Over the years the local inhabitants grew accustomed to the antics of strangers lured to these shores by visions of making swift fortunes. And thus it was in 1845 that a band of adventurers breezed along and set about constructing a breakwater across the mouth of the gully. Their theory was that holding back the ocean, pumping the pool dry at low tide and digging in the exposed sands would reward them with the dazzling sight of multitudes of shimmering coins, just begging to be harvested. They were favoured with unusually good weather at the construction stage, when a path was cut into the face of the cliff, iron rods were embedded in the rocks and the dam strengthened with baulks of timber. Just as the coffer dam was nearing completion, however, a south-westerly storm arose, destroying all their machinery and weeks of endeavour in one night.

If all this had caused local eyebrows to be raised, wry smiles were exchanged a couple of years later when a gang of tin miners arrived, with the novel notion of digging a dollar mine. The idea was to drill a vertical shaft down through the rock, then drive a 30 ft horizontal adit out under the sea, and let nature do the rest. For they figured that the force of the waves would loosen sand-bound dollars and obligingly force them along the adit and into the shaft, where they could be conveniently collected as and when conditions allowed. But, not surprisingly, this met with limited success. Things seemed to be going reasonably well until another south-westerly erupted, swamping the workings and destroying all their equipment. To add insult to injury, the miners were obliged to take to their heels to escape the perils of the deep.

Things were quiet for a while after these humiliating fiascos. Then, in 1872, a certain Mr Boyd became bitten with the treasure-seeking bug. His overall strategy was to capitalise on the existence of the earlier dollar mine, using more refined methods and harnessing the skills of miners, engineers and divers. Thus it was that a motley crew of professionals, aided and abetted by an assortment of seafaring jacks-of-all-trades and their faithful hounds, made a rip-roaring appearance on these isolated, windswept shores, and set about constructing a tented encampment, which they dubbed 'the Atlantic Hotel'. They were joined by an East London clergyman who happened to pass this way on vacation and became infected by their enthusiasm for this colourful enterprise, attracted by their cheerful camaraderie.

As they cleared the debris from the mine, they made the eerie discovery of tools and equipment, which their predecessors had abandoned in such desperate haste almost 30 years earlier. They were hampered all the way by bad weather, which created a particularly dangerous underswell at all states of the tide. But after a great deal of heavy toil, they succeeded in blasting away sections of rock and emplacing a large suction pump. This innovative apparatus was set in motion by the engine of a threshing machine, which was perched precariously on the cliff above. However, there was a hitch when the indiarubber driving bands caught against the jagged cliff face, and more ingenuity was required to find a way of allowing them to drive freely, without re-positioning the heavy machinery and bringing the whole lot tumbling down the cliff. Having eventually accomplished all that, they eagerly awaited the rewarding sight of flashes of silver, as they set their technology in motion and sieved through vast quantities of sand.

They beavered away when the weather was fine, and retreated to their camp or the nearest beer house when it was not. These sterling counterparts of the gold-diggers of California, Australia or South Africa lived in harsh conditions in the open, washed in the sea and yarned around their evening camp-fire in the time-honoured style. If they were successful they might gain an edge over their landlubbing colleagues, with the prospect of retrieving beautifully crafted, instant treasure trove, rather than raw hunks of shiny rock. However, when it became obvious that those elusive dollars needed a little more enticement, they stepped up the role of the divers, who were elaborately kitted out in bulbous rubber trousers reaching to the neck, hefty, weighted rubber boots and globe-like brass helmets with window pieces in the front. As he descended the ladder placed against the wave-worn rock, the diver's life was firmly entrusted into the hands of his mates, who kept the air pumps going.

When the skills of the divers failed to draw the treasures of the deep, attentions were turned to the expertise of the miners, in a last-ditch attempt to achieve success. If carefully orchestrated, subtle means had failed to bring about the desired results, it was time for sheer brute force. So they decided to blow up the sea-bed with dynamite! Three holes were bored in the mine shaft many feet below the sea, and the dynamite and fuses carefully emplaced. Then it was a case of igniting the end of the rope and swarming up the cliff face before they got caught up in the blast. As the minutes ticked by they glanced at each other uneasily. Then it happened! It started with a low and ominous roar, like distant, subterranean thunder. Then it gained noisy momentum, and culminated in an ear splitting, mighty explosion, which sent a spectacular jet of water, rocks and debris high into the air. But feverish excitement gave way to a frustrating sense of anticlimax, for the follow up search beneath the sea by divers had to be abandoned

Tin miners try their luck at Dollar Cove

because of incompatible weather conditions. In the event all this vision and endeavour counted for nothing, and by a providential irony, a farmer from Winnianton, who passed this way shortly after their departure, was rewarded with the incidental discovery of two silver dollars.

Daunting as all this may seem, the failure of others apparently added a certain spice to successive generations of hankerers after Neptune's elusive hoard. Just two years later the *West Briton* reported that more businesslike attempts were to be made to recover the riches which lay beneath the cliffs of Halzephron. These had the blessing of the Board of Trade, as long as everything was done properly and they received a percentage of the finds. Coastguards were to be in attendance on the cliffs while raising work was being carried out, and any discoveries made were to be lodged in the hands of the Receiver of Wreck at Penzance. Professional divers, skilled in recovering treasures from wrecks all over the world were to be employed, and no one seemed to entertain the slightest doubt of the success of the enterprise, which involved an outlay of over £1,000.

The newspaper sounded a prophetic note, albeit a trifle prematurely, by relating this cautionary tale:

'Those of our readers who recollect the beautiful story of *Quadroona* will remember that after years of peril and hardship, and at last recovering the coveted treasure, the ship which brought it and the adventurers home was nearly wrecked through internal dissensions – a rock on which many a well-based enterprise has been shattered; and it is to be hoped that the founders of the dollar recovery scheme now in progress will exercise a wise discretion in deferring any operation until the terms of division of the immense riches, which seem certain to be salved, are clearly defined.'

The renewed interest in the 'Dollar Wreck' was generated by Mr John Toy, an ironmonger of Helston, who had combed the area regularly and made occasional finds, and whose son claimed to have seen a huge iron treasure chest lying on the bed of the ocean at Gunwalloe. The scheme, backed by Vivian, Grylls & Kendall, bankers of Helston, who were selling shares at £3 a time, pointed out to hopeful clients that a number of treasure ships had spilled their specie on these shores. They were confident that their methods, employing experienced divers working inside an iron caisson, would succeed where other attempts had failed. But, despite all these well laid plans, they found nothing in the first season, and although they achieved a modicum of success the following year, the scheme was not viable, and the company went into voluntary liquidation.

This disappointing outcome did not prevent divers and reckless adventurers trying their luck with a variety of ingenious devices, such as salvage vessels anchoring close inshore, laying pipes on the sea-bed, and pumping for all they were worth. But Neptune shrugged off these attempts, and, indeed, many a hopeful Jolly Jack Tar was lucky to escape with his life. In more recent times, Dollar Cove has been the haunt of sub-aqua divers, who arrived with great expectations, but left empty-handed. However, local treasure hunter Roland Morris, who claimed to have located the Dollar Wreck in 1978, after four years of searching, had a dispute with the National Trust in regard to the rights of the wreck. So he called off the planned treasure hunt and never revealed the whereabouts of the sunken ship.

On 12th June 1992 the *Western Morning News* reported:

'Cornish treasure hunter Roland Morris has died in a Penzance nursing home, taking to the grave the secret of one of Britain's most famous shipwrecks.'

8

The *Mohegan* Disaster

◆

They say that it is unlucky to change the name of a ship. Back in 1897, the 6,889 ton steel-screw steamship, which started life as the *Cleopatra*, was one of five vessels being constructed at Earle's, at their yard in Hull, for Wilson & Sons. This splendid steamer, registered A1 at Lloyd's, incorporated some of the most sophisticated technology of the time, with the emphasis firmly on safety at sea. For, in the event of an emergency, she should have experienced the benefits of her eight watertight bulkheads, her fail-safe lighting and pumping systems, backed up with the security of eight lifeboats, conveniently suspended on davits fitted with theoretically fast and efficient lowering gear, and each capable of bearing 59 passengers. She also carried three compasses.

As it happened, this fleet of ships was acquired by the Atlantic Transport Company before the *Cleopatra* was launched and, although her new owners wanted to rename her the *Mohegan*, she made her maiden voyage as the *Cleopatra*. If renaming a ship does, indeed, augur ill, the portents were there right from the start. Having left Hull on 29th July 1898, for London, her first voyage across the Atlantic was beset with teething troubles, mostly connected with the new water system feeding her boilers. If this was a disappointing beginning, worse was to come, for she took 20 days to limp back from New York to London and needed an immediate overhaul. When this comprehensive work was completed the Board of Trade checked her compasses and tested her lifeboat efficiency, and it was claimed that eight men could lower and raise the ship's boats in five minutes. After this she was officially renamed the *Mohegan*. Although her new name appeared boldly in brass upon her handsome bows, the ship's bell still bore testimony to her original name (and some would say her original nature).

When the *Mohegan* sailed down the Thames on 13th October, carrying ninety-six crewmen, six cattlemen, fifty-three First Class passengers and a mixed cargo, the Trinity House pilot, who left the vessel after taking her round North Foreland, considered her to have been in good trim. If some of the wealthy passengers were wishing for terra firma as they encountered a stiffening breeze in the Channel, their stylish surroundings and the sight of their captain, cutting a salty dash as a fine figure of a British seafaring man, inspired their confidence. And, indeed, Captain Robert Griffiths, an experienced old sea-dog, aged 42 years or so, later described as a man of good nerve and perfectly sober habits, was also the Commodore of the line, entrusted with their finest ships.

But as the *Mohegan* progressed down the Channel at a steady 13 knots, some experienced seamen and seasoned passengers began to notice things which they found slightly disturbing. Early in the voyage the second engineer felt uneasy that normal lifeboat procedure, with the allocating of lifeboat stations, had not been carried out as would have been expected. Discerning passengers commented about the apparent slackness of some of the officers who were walking around smoking cigarettes. Failure of the electric lighting system had resulted in the novelty of dinner by candlelight. However, the most immediate and disturbing thing was that the Eddystone Lighthouse seemed to be in the wrong position, and the land appeared to be getting too close. Quartermaster John Juddery, who was on his first voyage with the *Mohegan* and who took turns at the wheel, became increasingly worried about this, but he had to adhere to the orders of his superiors. When quartermaster Frederick Butt, under the watch of second officer Edward Cole, handed over to quartermaster George August, saying 'West-by-North,' and his colleague affirmed 'West-by-North it is,' their fate was sealed.

Just after lunch it had been a case of 'All's well', as the *Mohegan* passed Prawle Point Signal Station, then Joseph Burnfield, a signalman at Rame Head, had sighted her less than ten miles from the shore. Off-duty customs officer, Mr Fooks, who was walking near Pendennis Point with his daughter thought it was odd when a large vessel, which seemed to be making for Falmouth harbour at a speed of about 13 knots, careered on towards the entrance of the Helford river. The sight of the *Mohegan* on her perilous course caused great consternation on the Lizard shore, and the Coverack coastguard fired a warning rocket in an attempt to alert them to the danger. It seemed to him that she veered slightly in an effort to rectify the situation. But it was too late. James Hill, coxswain of the Porthoustock lifeboat, who happened to be standing at his door just before 7 pm, could not believe his eyes when he saw the vessel proceeding rapidly, with all lights ablaze, on a collision course with the deadly Manacle Rocks. 'She's coming right in!' he yelled in horror, and rushed to summon his crew.

If the ill-fated *Mohegan* had attempted to veer to port, she was travelling too fast to retrieve the situation. We shall never know whether eventual realisation of impending danger was in response to the urgent signals from the shore, or whether the old Manacle Bell gave a foretaste of doom. Be that as it may, a few seconds before 6.50 pm, there was a sudden order for the engines to be stopped. The third engineer, William Ferguson, who had come on duty at 6 pm, was taken aback by this abrupt message, which was almost instantly followed by a slight shock, and escalating scraping noises from beneath the keel. Everybody aboard was startled by the alarming scrunching sounds, which erupted into a sickening climax, as if the bottom of the vessel were being ripped out by relentless, jagged rocks.

The appalling truth was that the *Mohegan* had run at full speed onto the Maen Varses, an outer section of the sharp and deadly Manacles Reef, which had been the scene of countless shipwrecks over the centuries. The result of the impact was such that water started rushing into the engine-room from all directions, lifting up the metal floor plates and flooding it to a depth of 3 ft in less than a minute. Ferguson shouted frantically for the valves on the boilers to be eased, to let off steam. Then the gauge glasses shattered, and the crew made a rush for the deck. The electric light appliances on the second platform were soon submerged, and then the whole vessel was plunged into darkness. This made the horror of the situation even more terrifying for all concerned, as the stricken ship swayed in the surf, ground on the rocks and became continually washed out by the big breakers. Having struck in Number 1 or Number 2 hold, forward on the starboard side, the forward section of the ship began to settle, and she listed to port, then more heavily to starboard. Distress rockets fired from the ship were answered by others exploding from the shore. Shrieks and terrified cries of the passengers filled the air. The anguished captain knew that help was coming, but would it arrive in time? He knew that his first priority must be to get the ship's own lifeboats launched.

Many of the smart passengers were putting on their gladrags or were already seated in the dining-room when the cruel crunch came. Most people instinctively rushed for the deck and were appalled to discover that their prestigious ship was wrecked upon the rocks. And then the lights went out, making bids for cool-headedness and survival well nigh impossible. There were conflicting reports about the way the captain and his officers handled the emergency, and some incredibly harrowing ones about the plight of individuals, particularly young children, thereafter. Some of the crew stood by the lifeboats, giving priority to women and children. But there was a delay in getting them launched, partly due to the vessel's heavy list to starboard. In the event, only two were launched before the ship finally foundered, and one of them swamped and capsized.

Only 20 minutes elapsed between the striking of the vessel and her foundering, during which time the mass of terrified humanity aboard the sinking ship was part of a scene of the utmost, poignant pathos that could ever be imagined. There were heart-rending pleas from mothers, on behalf of their offspring, and cries for help from little children who said they did not want to die yet. It was said that the captain, wearing a lifebelt around his waist and another around his hips, jumped overboard as the ship, with her stern high in the air, gave her last lurch and slid beneath the waves, leaving her masts and funnel protruding somewhat incongruously above the surface of the waves.

It was about seven o'clock when the firing of the assembly rocket at the Porthoustock Lifeboat Station notified the district that a shipping disaster had occurred, and people hurried down to the coast from all quarters. The lifeboat *Charlotte* was launched within half an hour. One of the crewmen said:

'As we pulled out from the cove we could see nothing, and we cruised down the coast. Soon, however, we heard shouts and cries for help, and, after pulling some distance, we came upon a boat, keel up, with two or three men clinging to it. We managed to get two into our boat with great difficulty, but the third fell off and disappeared. We pulled on further, and could still hear shouts and cries, and soon we came upon another boat bottom up with two men clinging to it. By this time we had found out that there was a big wreck, and we signalled for further help. These two men were got on board, but we could still hear cries, which seemed to proceed from under the boat, and the rescued men said they believed there were several underneath. With great exertion and trouble we got a grapnel under the side and righted her. To our surprise we found that not only were there several people in her, but two or three were alive. Amongst them was a woman whom we rescued, and found that she had badly injured her ankle, and who afterwards told De Leverton Spry that she had been clinging to the under part of the boat for hours. We next came upon a boat full of men and only one woman, and with these we returned to the shore, making twenty-eight in all, so that we could pull only four oars a side, instead of six. After we had started to return we came upon a lady alone on a plank, whom we rescued. We pulled home as soon as possible and landed our living and dead cargo, one of the rescued having died on the way. On returning we found that after we started the Second Coxswain of the lifeboat and three volunteers, at very great risk, took the Doctor's boat and pulled out in the seething waves, and darkness to try and find the whereabouts of the wreck. This, after great exertion and peril, they

Captain Griffiths and the wreck of the 'Mohegan'

did, but could not get near enough to render any help because of the surf. They told us where she was, and we immediately pulled away again for the wreck, which we found with about four or five feet of the funnel and the four masts sticking out of the water. We took off twelve men and one woman from the mainmast, the cook and boatswain from the foremast, one seaman from the mizzen, and one poor fellow who was clinging by one hand to the funnel, his other hand having been badly smashed. It was now about 5 o'clock and, after being out from about 8 pm until 5 am, we had all of us had quite enough, and our Coxswain Hill would not leave until he made quite sure that there was not another living soul to be seen.'

The woman rescued from the plank was Miss Noble, a young passenger from Baltimore, and the one stoutly clinging to the mainmast was the assistant stewardess, Miss Piggott. Quartermaster John Juddery, who had been in the rigging of the mizzen-mast, bravely swam to the lifeboat and took a line back to the next mast, thereby allowing those clinging to the rigging and funnel to be rescued. The lifeboatmen then lifted their anchor, letting her drop while they took off the survivors. As the lifeboat came ashore for the last time, pent-up strain and tension erupted into rounds of cheering. The Porthoustock lifeboat had saved forty-four lives, while three other survivors had been miraculously saved in the same vicinity.

In the sombre and harrowing scenes which followed, the local folk demonstrated true Christianity in action, helping to deal with the appalling situation of the dead, who continued to be washed in on the tide, laying them out reverently in cottages, in the boathouse and inside the parish church. They threw their dwellings open to the survivors, many of whom were badly injured, ministering to their needs, and harnessing the knowledge, experience and practical help of the much respected Shipwrecked Mariners' Society. Many of these shocked survivors had a rare and fascinating tale to tell of initiative, fortitude, endurance and courage. That prepossessing young lady, Miss Noble, who appeared most bright and cheerful despite all the distressing circumstances, told how she had been at dinner when she suddenly felt a rising of the vessel, accompanied by a grating sound. Several people had exclaimed 'What's that?' or 'We're ashore!' and everyone made a rush for the deck. Realising that this was an emergency, Miss Noble returned to her cabin to grab a jacket and stuff a few valuables into her pocket, and all the lights had gone out by the time she was back on deck. The Fourth Officer placed a lifebelt on her and some of the other ladies, and urged them to get into the lifeboat, which the sailors were having difficulty in launching. 'I can hardly remember what happened next,' she said. 'But suddenly I was washed overboard and found myself struggling in the sea. I am accustomed to the sea and did not feel very frightened. Quite close to me was the Fourth Officer, who assisted me to reach a plank, and during the next four hours of fighting for life we remained together on the plank, and owing to his help and cheering words I feel I owe my life. How we became separated I cannot say; but suddenly I found myself alone, but clinging to the plank until rescued by the lifeboat, about 6 o'clock in the morning. Shortly before I missed him he told me to hold tight, as we were near the shore, and might get washed off.'

Miss Maud Roudebush, a young American actress, had the doubly tragic experience of losing her beloved mother in the course of the shipwreck, in particularly pitiful circumstances. They found themselves in company with others, including the supposedly frail Mrs Compton Swift, who had been travelling with her physician (an early victim of the shipwreck), in one of the ship's boats. A rope fastening at one end had severed, leaving the lifeboat swaying precariously, until it overturned. Miss Roudebush and Mrs Swift were trapped underneath, but they clung to their seats for over an hour, their bodies suspended in the water. When help came, the lifeboatmen mistook Mrs Swift for a corpse, but she protested loudly, and was cut free with an axe. Miss Roudebush said she had managed to keep herself alive by screaming, but was heart-broken to discover that her mother had died on her way to the shore, and she had her mother's body removed from the boathouse to a cottage before having it shipped back to New York with her.

When the vessel filled, George Maule, a shipper of horses, grabbed a lifebelt and jumped overboard in company with Mr Couch, the chief officer, who told him to dispense with his coat and boots, which would drag him under. George Maule managed to find a piece of plank, which he clung to for eight hours, before being picked up by the tug *Penguin*, from Falmouth. But Mr Couch, like the rest of the officers, was lost. Able seaman William Moore jumped overboard with all his clothes on, then, after swimming around for a while, came across one of the ship's lifeboats, which was empty. He pulled away with one oar, and managed to get a shipmate aboard, who was lying exhausted on a raft. The sea was running rather heavily, and the boat was filling with water. It was eventually dashed to pieces on the rocks, then they were flung on the rocky shore. They lay there, bruised and battered, until being rescued and taken up the steep hill to St Keverne in a cart.

Mr Ernest Arthur Leeston Smith, a smart young American, lean and pale, owed his survival to the fact that he was a champion swimmer. After the bugle had summoned him to dinner, he was returning to his cabin to dress when he heard a tremendous crash, then the sound of breaking china in the saloon, and feared there had been a collision. When he realised that the situation was so serious, he rushed down to his cabin – Number 13 – to get a lifebelt, and discovered it was about a foot deep in water. Then he rushed back on deck, secured his lifebelt, and started to crawl up the mast. But when he realised that the ship was going down, he made a rapid descent and as he tore along the deck, he realised that the captain was sprinting along beside him. They plunged into the water together as the ship gave her final, sickening lurch, and struck out through the troubled sea, filled with screaming, half demented human beings and corpses. Some of the panic-stricken victims grabbed hold of him and nearly dragged him under. Then the remainder of the passengers, who had ranged themselves along the side of the ship, all seemed to plunge overboard together, and most of them disappeared for ever beneath the mighty wave which followed. The courageous lad kept swimming until he got sucked under a large rock, but somehow he managed to get free. He kept swimming about until he came across a kind of raft, with a rough sail, and he managed to haul himself onto it. Although he was thrown off again and again, sometimes being tossed into the air, his determination to survive was such that he was able to scramble back. Then the edge of the raft got caught in the cleft of a rock, and he was catapulted right over the top. Nothing daunted, he kept on swimming until he reached the safety of the shore, about two and a half miles from the scene of the shipwreck.

William Ferguson, who had been in the engine-room when the vessel struck and who had been injured in getting the lifeboats out, described the water rushing over the decks of the stricken ship just before she went down. He jumped overboard and while he was in the water he saw a lifeboat swamp and capsize, with the loss of about 30 men, women and children, and another lifeboat which was floating about, keel uppermost. After threshing around for a bit, he was able to catch hold of the whistle pipes close to the funnel. As it happened, he was the last survivor to be plucked from the wreck by the Porthoustock lifeboat.

For this heroic rescue, the coxswain, James Hill, was awarded the Silver Medal of the RNLI, and the quartermaster, John Juddery, received the Silver Medal of the Board of Trade in recognition of his gallant conduct. There were various expressions of heartfelt gratitude and a memorial window was subsequently placed in St Keverne church. Some of the shipwrecked victims were embalmed and returned to the United States, but most lie in a mass grave near the north door of the church, beneath a great cross, simply inscribed '*Mohegan*'.

After much deliberation the Court of Inquiry came to the conclusion that the *Mohegan* had been on a very wrong course, but as the captain and all his officers were lost in the disaster, no one will ever know how she came to be so far from her proper course as to run headlong onto the notorious *Manacles*. But, many years later, Commander John Rowe, who had sailed on many of the old sailing ships as well as commanding vessels in the First and Second World Wars, asked the former captain of the ship which became the *Mohegan* what he thought about her. 'Well, John,' he said, 'She was a whore by name, and a whore by nature!'

9

The Fate of the *Bencoolen*

◆

'The grandeur of the sea during storms can in few places be more impressive than at Bude, and how liable it is to storms will be sufficiently indicated when we mention that it is a common thing for vessels to be unable to quit or enter the haven for weeks together. Three months and more have occasionally occurred during which no seaman dared to venture his craft across the bar . . .'
(Thorough Guide North Devon & North Cornwall: *1899*).

It was said that the barque *Bencoolen*, one of a large fleet of Bengal traders owned by Edward Bates & Company of Liverpoool, was seaworthy and in good order when she left Liverpool, bound for Bombay, on 13th October 1862, with a crew of 32. John Jones, the manager of this vessel, which had been constructed seven years earlier at St Johns, New Brunswick, spoke highly of the captain, who had been in his employ for over six years. 'Captain Chambers had always been a good and efficient seaman, of sober habits,' he declared, 'trustworthy in every sense of the word.' Be that as it may, this fully-rigged three-masted ship, of 1,415 tons burthen, carrying a general cargo, including telegraph poles and a large quantity of iron ran into difficulties soon after leaving Liverpool, and some said that the captain had not been entirely sober since they had left port.

There was a fresh west-south-westerly breeze blowing as the impressive vessel sailed out of Liverpoool and, as this veered to the south and reached gale force, the large wooden barque with her three iron masts was having a rough time of it in the Irish Sea. The winds intensified on the fourth night out, then disaster struck. The heavy foremast came down with a run, carrying away two sailors working aloft and fouling the main and mizzen-masts, causing them to snap off close to the deck. Thus a stately-looking vessel was reduced to a helpless wreck within the space of a few minutes, and continued to drift hither and thither at the behest of the hostile elements until she finally met her doom.

At a time when a crew looked to its captain for direction, discipline and reassurance, the person who should have fulfilled this courageous function, was seeking refuge from these harsh realities in increasing amounts of alcohol, and some of the crew started following his example. Chief Officer Powell, who had been badly injured by a falling block when the mast fell, remained sober, but unable to give much of a lead. So those with sufficient strength of character assumed responsibility. The vessel was taking in water, and it was a case of all available hands to the pumps, while others used their ingenuity in constructing a raft from spare spars and fragments of wreckage, as the ship's boat had been rendered useless by the falling yards. For this might well be their only chance of salvation.

In the early dawning of 21st October, when the wind had veered north-north-west, watchers on the cliffs near Bude might have discerned the stricken vessel, which had been drifting helplessly since being dismasted 40 miles south of the Tuskar Rock in Southern Ireland. However, few would have credited what was going on aboard that once-stately barque.

James Mackay, the ship's carpenter, was in charge of the crippled Indiaman as she was being driven towards the shore, with about 5 ft of water in her hold. But whatever efforts were being made by the brave men aboard the *Bencoolen* were being hampered by the behaviour of her drunken captain, the steward and two seamen, who had also taken to the bottle. The situation grew increasingly tense, and shortly before the vessel struck, the steward loaded a musket with powder and ball, and threatened to shoot the inebriated crewmen, unless they calmed down and stopped quarrelling. Fearing that he might do so, and that the violence might escalate, seaman Henry Hollmann snatched the weapon from the steward's hands, flung it overboard, and hastily took refuge in what remained of the rigging.

In the early afternoon the drunken captain lost his grip and fell backwards as he was attempting to make his way down to his cabin, and the steward, who suddenly started sobering up in the face of imminent shipwreck, was ordered by the second mate to go below to assist him. However, the captain did not welcome such assistance, and he returned to the deck. The steward ordered one of the seamen to go below, but he similarly made a rapid reappearance on deck, saying that the captain refused to be disturbed. As their fate closed in on them, a few remained at the wheel under the command of James Mackay, and the rest sought refuge in the fo'c'sle head. Harbours of refuge were few and far between on this iron-bound coast, and Bude was not one of them.

The dismasted barque had been sighted off Bude about noon, making fast for the shore, under the influence of the strong winds then prevailing, and being buffeted around in mountainous seas. When first

The Steward of the 'Bencoolen' steadies the crew

observed, she had no sail whatever set upon her, but then a little square sail was seen to be set, and a flag of distress hoisted. It was reported at the time that signals from the shore directing them to make for Bude seemed to be understood by the crew. The vessel, which had a deep draught of 21 ft attempted to make for the harbour, but struck near the breakwater and fell broadside across the narrow channel at the entrance.

Here the *Bencoolen* lay, at the mercy of the raging surf, with sea after sea exploding across her deck in the most frightful manner, threatening to sweep the shipwrecked men overboard at any moment. Then a signal-board bearing the words 'KEEP ON BOARD' was hoisted from the shore; a directive nobly observed by the distressed mariners assembled on the stern, who waved their arms frantically and cried out for help. Efforts were made by the coastguards to establish contact from the shore by means of the rocket apparatus. But, as it happened, only two lines were available at the station at this crucial time, and attempts to fire these lines aboard were unsuccessful in these rough and windy conditions. So the lifeboat was brought down to the water's edge, and efforts were made to raise an experienced crew. Bude, unlike the other Cornish ports, had no fishing industry, and therefore no fishermen to man the lifeboat, as was traditionally the case. Instead, they had to rely on landsmen, canal men and any coastguards or sailors from vessels which happened to be in port at the time; men who had not had regular training in the specialist manning of the RNLI's lifeboats. On this occasion there were no ready volunteers, apart from some plucky canal workers and, by the time a crew had been mustered, valuable time had been lost. Conditions had deteriorated, and they considered it was now too dangerous for launching through such treacherous groundseas. Boatswain Thomas Aspinall said afterwards, 'We should have launched a raft, which we had previously made, earlier – if we had not seen the lifeboat, on which we relied for assistance, expecting that she would have come to us, and I am of the opinion that she might have done so in safety, when the vessel first struck.'

Crowds of people were assembled on the breakwater and neighbouring cliffs, but no one was able to render any assistance. It was a very harrowing scene as they stood there helplessly, watching their fellow human beings drowning before their very eyes. Several of the crew, including James Mackay, jumped overboard in a bid for freedom, and some saved their lives by doing so. Sadly, Mackay, who was a strong swimmer, got to the shore, but lost his life when his improvised line broke. The safety of the shore was tantalisingly close, and yet so inaccessible. Salvation was denied them by a barrier of thundering surf and a dangerous undercurrent. Those left on board turned their attentions to the raft, which they managed to launch with their injured chief officer and others lashed to it. The onlookers held their breath as the improvised bark and its mortal cargo was washed close to the shore, only to be swept out to sea again.

The West Briton of 14th November 1862 reported:

'It was now to be perceived that the raft was quite close to the cliffs on the north side of the harbour; the tide at this time breaking heavily against their base. A little creek, some thirty feet across, at the extreme end of the harbour, was full of fragments of timber, and into this the raft at last was washed, with several dead and only two living men lashed upon it. It took but a few minutes to run round the harbour; a line was passed down the cliff, and one by one twelve men, six living, six dead were drawn and hoisted up, as carefully as could be, and there laid upon the grass – so fearfully exhausted were those who still breathed, that only one could speak. These were immediately carried to the village. Those who seemed dead were rubbed upon the spot, and every man round eager and ready to do his best; one, we thought, gasped, but all exertions were in vain, and they were sent in dead.'

The massive barque did not hold together very long, after being driven on shore at Bude, and wreckage was strewn all along the coast. Only six of the remaining thirty crewmen who had survived thus far, lived to tell the tale. The remainder met with a watery grave, as countless other seafarers along this formidable section of coast had done before them. Those who survived the ordeal were treated kindly by Sir T.D. Acland and Mr Maskell, but had to face the distressing task of identifying their fellow crewmen. It was heart-rending and sickening for those who had to deal with the aftermath of the shipwreck, which included coping with the mangled, bloody bodies which the sea yielded up. They were removed in carts and laid out in the boathouse.

This sad and lamentable affair cast a heavy gloom throughout the whole neighbourhood, and no one who experienced that catastrophic day would ever forget it. They placed the figurehead of the wrecked ship in the cemetery, and a monumental stone inscribed:

'HERE LIE DEPOSITED

The Remains of the Chief Mate and Thirteen Seamen, a portion of the crew of the *Bencoolen*, which was wrecked at the entrance to this Harbour.

October 21st, 1862'

A guidebook of 1884 tells us that there was scarcely a garden which was not embellished with the figurehead or some other part of many a gallant ship that had been hurled upon this fatal coast, and that many relics of the *Bencoolen* stood in the locality as sad mementoes of this tragic event. Indeed, the catastrophe is recalled in Bude today, with the naming of streets and artefacts in the museum.

If any good can be said to have come out of this disastrous shipwreck, perhaps it was that the RNLI recognised the particular local problems at Bude in regard to availability of suitable crew, and problems in launching through the ever-present surf at the shallow mouth of the limited harbour. They provided a new coxswain and the nucleus of an efficient crew, as well as a new lifeboat. The criticism of this station (made mostly by those who had never manned a lifeboat) was unfortunate, for its lifeboatmen had been awarded twelve Silver Medals between 1845 and 1881, three of them to the fearless and famous coastguard, Henry Tregidgo. The young lifeboatmen of today, who are only too aware of the capricious nature of these waters, must identify closely with their forebears as they brave the hazards of turbulent surf and groundseas and suddenly erupting storms, in their inshore lifeboat, very close to the elements.

10

The Voyage of the *Mystery*

♦

Outside the Fishermen's Mission in Newlyn is a plaque depicting a Cornish lugger, recalling an epic seafaring adventure of 1854. And therein hangs a heartening tale of youthful enterprise, courage and vision.

In the middle of the last century, when Gold Rush fever was at its height, the heady prospect of making a quick fortune, not to mention the romance and adventure of pastures new, struck an enthusiastic, pioneering chord with many a young man, particularly in Cornwall where the traditions of mining were so strong. Indeed, the local newspapers of the day carried the most alluring advertisements from shipping companies, who vied with each other to offer the most attractive and competitive deals in regard to passages to Australia. Shipping companies, such as the Liverpool Line, the White Star Line and the Black Ball Clipper Packets, which operated out of Liverpool, had agents based in Penzance. First class steamers, including the ill fated *Nile* (see 'Strange Happenings at Godrevy') and her sister ship *Lady Eglington*, were providing regular direct links with Penzance, Falmouth, Plymouth, Portsmouth and London. The publicity for these splendid, speedy, first class clipper ships, offering fares to Melbourne from 16 guineas upwards, pointed out that their captains were Gentlemen of great experience, that they carried recognised Surgeons and Chaplains, and also mentioned recreational pastimes such as Chess, Backgammon and Draughts.

A mail steamship, sailing from Southampton to Australia, in October 1854, offered a tempting deal for the more discerning passenger thus:

'The General Screw Steamship Company's Screw Steam ship *Argo*, 1,850 tons, 300 horse power, George Hyde Commander, will sail from Southampton with Her Majesty's Mails for Australia, Port Phillip & Sydney, on Wednesday, the 4th October, at two o'clock, p.m. punctually. The *Argo*, one of the finest ships afloat, is justly celebrated for her last passage to Australia, having made the run out in 64 days, and home within the same period. She is also the finest steamship that returned to England via Cape Horn, thus accomplishing a voyage round the world in 128 days. The vessels forming the superb fleet of screw steamers of this Company, of which this ship is one, are well known for their punctuality and speed with which their voyages are performed. No expense has been spared in the construction, and the accommodation they offer to the public is unsurpassed, if equalled, by any ships afloat. Rates of passage money vary according to the accommodation required, from 30 to 100 guineas.

Full particulars as to freight and passage may be had at the Company's Office, 27, Cannon St., London, or of Mr N.B. Downing, Penzance, Agent.'

However, shortly afterwards Mr Wilcocks, of Plymouth, reckoned he had cornered the lucrative local market when he announced that his magnificent new ship *George Marshall*, 2,300 tons, would set sail early in December, adding that she was expected to convey a 'West of England colony'.

The old-established Kelynack family of Newlyn, with a long tradition of fishing and seafaring, demonstrated initiative and a desire to be in the forefront of the action – not to mention a certain penchant for being in the limelight. Newlyn at this time was a small fishing settlement on the shore of Mount's Bay, with the inhabitants gleaning basic livelihoods by fishing, farming, tinning and smelting. So the young men cast their eyes to the far horizon and beyond for more fulfilling opportunities for their future. The ships which regularly passed these shores with worldly sailors and worldly riches, gave them a tantalising taste of what life could offer young men of energy and enterprise. Charles Kelynack had saved up enough money for a passage to Australia, and his colourful and exciting accounts of his exploits filled his family and friends back home with envy and longing.

These letters and the enticing advertisements in the press had captured the imagination of young Job Kelynack and his mates, who reckoned that the only chance they had of joining Charles in Australia was to sell the family-owned lugger *Mystery*. They would no doubt have done this and taken passages aboard one of the fast and stylish clipper ships, along with many another young adventurer, had not fate, in the shape of Captain Richard Nicholls, intervened. Captain Nicholls was a local man commanding a vessel in the Welsh trade, who happened to be home on leave at that time.

The story goes that the idea for this adventure was hatched as the ale flowed freely in a Penzance inn, after Captain Nicholls heard of the plan to sell the family lugger. 'Why sell the *Mystery*?' he asked. 'When

Large crowds cheered them on their way

all is said and done, you will have disposed of the biggest family asset, with the money released being swallowed up in the fare and other expenses.' 'Well, if we don't sell the 'ole lugger, wot 'ope 'ave we got o' ever gettin' to Australia?' asked the lads, reluctant to let visions of wealth, perpetual sunshine and a better life on the other side of the world, slip from their grasp. 'I've got a much better idea, which will get you to Australia, retaining your biggest asset,' replied Captain Nicholls, his eyes lighting up with enthusiasm. 'This old lugger is a sturdy built craft, capable of coping with the most daunting of conditions, as she has demonstrated admirably in her daily dicings around Land's End and the Lizard. I reckon that if she can stand that, she can withstand anything that the oceans of the world can throw at her.' 'That be so. But we don't 'ave the knowledge o' worldwide navigation, an' suchlike.' 'But *I* have. *You've* got the everyday handling skills, and *I* have the worldwide experience. Between the lot of us, I reckon we've got what it needs. Tell you what! I'll be your captain, if you'll be my crew!' The more they thought about this in the warm and mellowing atmosphere of the tavern, the more the idea appealed to them, as true sons of the sea. By the end of that evening, they were all fired with enthusiasm. If it all seemed a little hair-brained in the sober light of morning, none of the lads wanted to lose face by climbing down. The news spread like wildfire, and they determined to go through with the scheme.

The idea caused quite a stir around Newlyn, as work went ahead for the epic voyage. Adaptations were made to the craft, which was 36 ft long, 11 ft in the beam, with a draught of 6 ft. These included decking her fore and aft and sheathing her bottom with zinc. She looked smart as she emerged from the refit, with the number '233' emblazoned on her bow and on her sails. After she was launched she was loaded up with enough provisions to last four months, including the time-honoured hard tack (ships' biscuits), salted beef and a supply of fresh water, which also acted as ballast.

On 15th November, *The Cornish Telegraph* reported:

'A Mount's Bay Fishing Boat of only 16 tons, the *Mystery* of Newlyn, Captain Richard Nicholls, now lies within a short distance, ready to sail for Australia . . . The navigation of thousands of miles of ocean by such a craft is a great undertaking, and its success or failure will be looked for with considerable interest.'

Excitement mounted as Captain Nicholls and his youthful crew, consisting of Job Kelynack, William and Richard Badcock, Charlie Boase, Philip Curnow Mathews and Lewis Lewis prepared to leave harbour. Large crowds had assembled here, and along the cliffs, to wish them *bon voyage* and cheer them on their way. And who can imagine how their loved ones felt as the time of parting drew nigh, with cheerful bantering and last minute panics? For some of the crew were still in their teens.

The Cornish Telegraph of 22nd November reported:

'The *Mystery* fishing boat, which at the date of our last publication was only waiting for a favourable breeze to leave Mount's Bay for Melbourne, sailed at 3 o'clock on Saturday morning last – her crew in the best of health and spirits, and sanguine of a safe and speedy voyage. The wind at the time blew from the NE, the sails were set by friends of the voyagers, who accompanied them on board, and the *Mystery* started gallantly with the best wishes of acquaintances and onlookers, for her success.'

This apparently vulnerable little craft sailed on 18th November, just a few days before the recently launched, splendid screw steamship *Nile*, which carried passengers from the south coast to and from the world-wide clipper ships sailing in and out of Liverpoool, came to grief at Godrevy. For the fishermen who crewed the sturdy *Mystery*, a compass, sextant, barometer and generations of inherited seamanship were their only aids as they left these shores. The weather was fine for the first part of the voyage, as they sailed past Ushant, through the Bay of Biscay, passed Finistère and out into the Atlantic.

On 6th December *The Cornish Telegraph* reported:

'The *Mystery*, Newlyn fishing craft was spoken with by the Schooner *Eliza* (Sawyer) from Lisbon for Glasgow, on the 22nd ult. in lat. 41.46N. and longitude 13.55.W. Her crew were all well, and she was spanking along at the rate of eight knots an hour. Mr Richard Philps, of Plymouth, agent there for the *Shipping & Mercantile Gazette*, besides communicating that fact to the paper, kindly wrote the agent here, Mr W.D. Mathews on the subject. The *Mystery* must have been somewhere near Oporto – having made good progress, we should say.'

They reached Madeira at noon on 25th November, and the following day made contact with the men aboard the brig *St Vincent*, outward bound from the Cape of Good Hope, from Liverpool. Shortly after this they saluted flags with an English barque.

On 3rd December they reached the islands of San Antonia. Then they found themselves in the doldrums, and relieved their frustration by taking turns in scraping the ship's punt, which was lashed to the deck, with penknives. This also gave them the opportunity to do some leisurely fishing, which meant the luxury of eating fresh food, as distinct from their usual salty fare. Thus the fishing boat *Mystery* made her slow progress southwards, until her canvas filled out with the welcome trade winds. The lads from Newlyn had dreamed of sunny days at sea, but as they neared the Equator, the searing heat became hard to bear. But their attention was diverted from this when they suddenly hit heavy weather, and the jib split. However, there was some elation when they crossed the Equator on 15th December, with perhaps a lump or two in the throat as they thought of the folks back home preparing for a cool Christmas, without them.

The crew experienced variable weather on the way down to Trinidad and Martin Veza's Rocks, and they were able to make contact with the brig *Callao*, bound for Liverpool from South America, which carried a letter back to England for them. When the *Mystery* first arrived in Cape Town on 17th January, she was mistaken for one of the Table Bay cutters. Then the Harbour Master saw her being hauled up on the beach to have the barnacles scraped from her bottom, and went to investigate. The exciting news spread like wildfire throughout Cape Town, and the enthusiastic townsfolk gave them a welcome they would never forget. The shy lads from Newlyn found themselves celebrities; they were invited here, there and everywhere, and on the following Sunday they attended Divine Service aboard the British warship *Seringapatam*, which was under the command of Commodore Trotter.

Their welcome break in Cape Town allowed them to stock up with fresh provisions, and to post and collect their mail. In the event, the folks back home had to wait four months for news of their safe arrival in Cape Town. When the young adventurers left the port a week later, for the last lap of the voyage, they were given a terrific send-off by the people who had taken them to their hearts. Thus they sailed out of Cape Town to a veritable cacophony of sound, with cheers and the enthusiastic blending of ships' sirens re-echoing across the water. They also enjoyed the prestige of carrying the mails to Melbourne.

After leaving Cape Town, they ran into strong winds and heavy seas, which erupted into a hurricane, accompanied by torrential rain on 23rd February. This really put the lugger and her crew to the test. They pulled the *Mystery* hard into the wind, and let out the raft as a safety measure, for the anchored raft provided extra stability in these diabolical conditions, lessening the chances of a capsize. They hauled the raft aboard again when the winds moderated, but they were in for quite an exhilarating bounce for the rest of the way. They encountered snow storms and another hurricane on 5th March, when they rode to the raft for a second time. The raft was let out again on the 9th, when they had the added excitement of sighting the Australian mainland, land of their dreams, for the first time. They passed Cape Bridgewater on the 11th, Cape Otway on the 12th, and came to anchor in Hobson's Bay, Melbourne on the 14th March 1855. Thus they had accomplished this extraordinary enterprise in 116 days, which included the week spent in Cape Town.

A warm and well deserved welcome awaited them in Australia, and amongst those who greeted them and offered hospitality was Captain Price, RN, son of the famous Cornish squire Sir Rose Price, of Trengwainton, near their homes in Newlyn. A Cornishman's links with home are ever strong, and a miner from St Just in Penwith, who was working in the goldfields, cast speculation aside, for the sake of being on the coast in Melbourne to watch the arrival of the adventurers. The crew sent letters to their families and friends in Cornwall, but it was to be another four months before the news of their safe arrival in Australia was received.

Some say that the grass is always greener on the other side; some subscribe to the theory that it is better to travel in hope than to arrive. Although an experienced crew of Cornish fishermen with a proven, dependable fishing boat had arrived in a place teeming with fish and having a potentially lucrative market, things did not quite work out that way, although Captain Nicholls gave it a try. So the dear old *Mystery*, which had served them so well, was sold for £150 at Williamstown along with all their tackle. Sadly, she was later wrecked on the New Zealand shores. That was the fate of the Newlyn lugger *Mystery*; but what of her pioneering crew, now that they had actually reached the land of their dreams, which they had yearned for so much?

Captain Nicholls never got as far as the gold diggings, for he was back in Newlyn before the end of the year, pleased to resume his life as a skipper, serving various companies. It was a strange and sad irony that, after all his daredevil exploits, he was killed by a cab on the streets of London 13 years later. Job Kelynack was delighted to be reunited with his brother Charles at Bendigo. But Bendigo was very different from Newlyn. He felt the pull of his homeland, and decided to return there and live out the rest of his long and contented days as a fisherman.

When they reached Australia, the Badcock brothers decided that they did not wish to go digging for gold after all, so they both found employment in the Penal Service of Victoria, in charge of those who had also secured a free passage to Australia from the Old Country, albeit by courtesy of the Crown. William worked as a warder boatman, ferrying prisoners backwards and forwards from the convict hulks anchored out in the bay. This occupation had its hazards, as demonstrated on the occasion that some convicts attacked and killed the officer-in-charge, telling Badcock that he would go the same way, unless he kept his mouth shut. After being released from his post, he was happy to return to Newlyn with his brother and Job Kelynack, to resume the way of life that generations before them had known and loved. Charles Boase similarly felt moved to return to his roots in Cornwall.

Philip Curnow Mathews settled down in Australia, but he briefly revisited the land of his forefathers after the death of his wife, when he was able to persuade his niece in Mousehole to return to Australia with him, in order to look after his family. As for Lewis Lewis, he was content to remain in Australia until his dying day.

11

The Drama of the *Flying Enterprise*

◆

The historic port of Falmouth found itself the focus of worldwide attention in January 1952, as one of the most gripping sea dramas of modern times was enacted off the coast of Cornwall. But this epic tale of courageous men and their gallant battle with the raging elements, which captured everyone's imagination and mellowed into an all-time classic in the grand, heroic style, also left a mystery in its wake; and there was on-going speculation as to why the captain felt compelled to behave in the way he did.

The SS *Flying Enterprise*, a welded ship of 6,711 tons constructed in 1944, was originally named the *Cape Kumukaki*. But after the Second World War, the United States Maritime Commission sold her to the Isbrandtsen Line of New York, and she was given a new name, with an optimistic ring about it.

It was foggy as the *Flying Enterprise* left Hamburg on 21st December 1951, bound for New York, said to be carrying a mixed cargo of pig-iron, graphite, typewriters, violins, pickled onions, gherkins, bird cages, coffee, *objets d'art*, mail and Volkswagen cars. Then she ran into bad weather as she left the mouth of the Elbe and entered the North Sea. Most of the passengers had lost their enthusiasm for the Christmas Eve festivities as they made their way westwards down the English Channel, encountering south-westerly winds force 6 to 8 on the Beaufort scale. If 37 year old Captain Henrik Kurt Carlsen seemed particularly edgy, this might be attributed to the fact that the Volkswagens in the hold, which had not been crated, were in danger of breaking loose. They were all thankful when the winds veered and moderated a little on Christmas Day. But next morning the *Flying Enterprise* encountered south-westerly and west-south-westerly winds, rising force 8 to 10. This had increased to force 10 or 11 by six o'clock that evening, when ships in the area were finding themselves in trouble, and reporting waves of 30 ft or more, confused seas and violent squalls.

In conditions like these, waves with a length of about 500 ft caused considerable stress on a vessel of 396 ft and, on 27th December, she developed a crack on each side of her hull. Captain Carlsen later declared that the first hint of trouble came when the top deck split with a loud bang, like the sound of a pistol shot. The fissure was filled with cement and strengthened with heavy steel hawsers. Then the breaking of the rudder stock by an exceptionally heavy sea hastened an exceptional sequence of events. Water flooded the engine-room and caused the cargo to shift. The vessel developed a 30° list to port and, with her generator out of action, started to drift. Captain Carlsen recalled, 'We were doing all right until dawn the next day, when another cyclonic storm came up with some terrific seas. It was nothing but sea and water all over the place. With a broken ship I could not steer. One tremendous sea knocked her off course.' By this time he had no alternative but to send out a distress call and order the passengers and crew on deck.

At 12.53 pm GMT on 28th December, Land's End Radio received the urgency signal XXX from the steamer *General A.W. Greely*, relaying the following message from the SS *Flying Enterprise*, 'Encountering severe hurricane in lat. 49 20 N, long. 17 20 W, situation grave, have 30 deg. port list and just drifting. Ships in vicinity please indicate.' Shipping in the area responded to this call, the Norwegian tanker *Westfal Larsen* made her way to the casualty, and at 3.16 pm the motor vessel *Sherborne* sent a message to the *Flying Enterprise* that she was proceeding towards her at the utmost speed and hoped to be there within six hours, weather conditions permitting. Sixteen minutes later the *Flying Enterprise* put out the message: 'In same position. Please note XXX (urgency signal), now SOS.' The owners in New York requested towage assistance.

There was no ceasing of distress working. By seven o'clock the steamer *Southland* had got to within a mile of the casualty, while the *Sherborne* was three miles off. At 10.20 pm *Sherborne* reported, 'Dutch motor vessel *Noordam P.G.H.P.* now standing by with us, and steamer *Southland*.' As there was no change in the situation of the *Flying Enterprise*, it was hoped that she might stay afloat until daybreak, before transferring the passengers and crew, for it was certain to be a very dicey business in such hazardous conditions.

By dawn on 29th December the wind had decreased to force 7 or 8 and was generally between NW and SSW, but the plight of the vessel had become more acute. Captain Carlsen had to make the most momentous decision that any captain, responsible for his ship and all who sail in her, ever has to make; the order for everyone to abandon ship. It must have been an agonising dilemma, for many might perish in the process, but many more might be lost if they remained aboard and the ship went down, sucking them under as it went.

At 11.26 am the steamer *General A.W. Greely* reported, 'Steamer *War Hawk*, motor vessel *Sherborne* and steamer *Southland* alongside steamer *Flying Enterprise*, now taking off passengers and crew.' This process had been infinitely more difficult than this curt report implied. After experiencing problems in getting them off the disabled ship in these stormy conditions, during which time five boats from the rescue ships capsized, became swamped or otherwise disabled, the *Westfal Larsen* pumped out about 500 tons of her cargo of oil, thereby creating a calming effect by pouring oil on troubled waters. This enabled the ships' boats, including one from the *Sherborne*, to proceed with the rescue operations, and 37 lives were thus saved. The weather was bad, and deteriorating all the time. After all the passengers and crew had been taken off the stricken vessel, it was reported that Captain Carlsen would remain aboard on his own, until the arrival of a tug, which was on its way from Falmouth. The *Flying Enterprise* had a 60° list to port, rolling to 80°, but the captain reckoned she would hold out until the tug arrived. In the meantime, the *General A. W. Greely* would stand by. The captain sent his most sincere thanks to all the ships which had taken part in the rescue work. Little did they know then that, for the next 14 days, the whole world would identify with the brave drama about to be enacted. The gallant captain, photographed waving from the shelving deck of his storm-tossed ship, occupied the front pages of every newspaper. It was seen as a real life, thrilling adventure in the best traditions of the sea, with the heroic captain steadfastly refusing to leave his sinking ship.

Captain Carlsen remained in contact with the outside world with an emergency transmitter, and his first message to Captain Olsen, of the *General A.W. Greely* was, 'Will, of course stay on board until she makes port or goes down.' In fact, at that time, Carlsen could not in all conscience have abandoned his ship, for there seemed a reasonable chance that she might be safely towed into port. Deserting his ship would have far-reaching implications in regard to salvage rights. Dutch sources reported that the cargo was insured for a million dollars, and the company had insured the vessel for an additional quarter of a million dollars in the event of a total loss. Furthermore, there was on-going speculation about the true nature of the cargo, with mutterings about zirconium and components for the nuclear submarine *Nautilus*.

The owners, who had been aware of the split hull on the 27th, had called for towage assistance to take the vessel to the United Kingdom on the 28th. On the 30th L. Smit & Co. reported that the Dutch tug *Oceaan* had passed the Lizard at 4 pm and was proceeding westwards, having been engaged under Lloyd's Form of Salvage Agreement. But, as it happened, she was diverted to go to the aid of the tug *Zwarte Zee*. Later that day it was reported that the tug *Turmoil* would be proceeding towards the casualty, as soon as she had disposed of her present tow.

On New Year's Day, the American steamer *Southland* arrived in Rotterdam with eight passengers and eight crewmen from the *Flying Enterprise*. Meanwhile, the United States destroyer *John W. Weeks* was proceeding towards the casualty, which was now 245 miles south-west of Fastnet. She was now flooded in Number 3 hold and her decks were awash to the hatch combings on the port side. But, despite this, the captain of the *Golden Eagle* reckoned that she had a good chance of remaining afloat. On 2nd January the destroyer *John W. Weeks* relieved the US naval supply ship *Golden Eagle*, which had been keeping watch over the helpless vessel, and communication was established with Carlsen by radio telephone. He was said to be in good health and spirits. Commander W.L. Thompson mentioned very heavy weather, very rough seas and a barometer, already low, falling steadily.

The plight of this courageous captain, alone aboard his stricken vessel in the storm-lashed Atlantic, with other vessels hovering in the vicinity and aircraft circling overhead, seemed to be the nucleus of world attention, touching everyone and generating goodwill and a positive desire for him to emerge triumphant. While awaiting the arrival of the tug, Carlsen set up camp in the radio cabin, so as to remain in close contact with the outside world. It was difficult for him to move around the heavily-listing ship in a topsy-turvy situation where bulkheads were angled like decks, and decks had taken the place of the bulkheads. In order to reach a food supply, he had to crawl along sections of the ship which were poised crazily, and for the first day or so he sustained himself on Christmas cake and beer. He recognised the importance of sleep in this situation, and filled an area between the bulkhead and the settee with blankets, to create a reasonably level resting place.

Excitement had been mounting in Falmouth, where the *Falmouth Packet* newspaper spoke of a week of gales and the port's role in a number of sea dramas, 'Spotlight of national publicity has been focused on the Falmouth-based ocean-going tug *Turmoil*, which reached Falmouth Bay with *Mactra* in tow, then made a swift turnaround to go to the aid of the American freighter *Flying Enterprise*, lying with a heavy list 350 miles off Land's End, with her brave captain aboard.' The *Turmoil*, one of the world's largest and most powerful tugs, which had left Falmouth harbour full-speed-ahead on 2nd January 1952, took almost two days to reach the casualty.

Just before making contact with the *Flying Enterprise*, Captain

Parker of the tug *Turmoil* sent a message via Land's End Radio, 'Expect to arrive *Enterprise* 2100 hours tonight. Speed at present 13 knots. In moderate weather with heavy swell still running. Have high hopes of connecting towing gear tonight, having once viewed the situation of freighter on arrival. Due to trim of vessel intentions are to tow her stern first, with port of destination remaining in abeyance and dependent upon prevailing weather. If possible do not intend sending a boarding party. Method of connecting with only Captain Carlsen aboard has been decided upon. Searchlights will be used.' The steamer was then drifting in a south-easterly direction at a speed of about 1.7 knots.

The tug *Turmoil* arrived on the scene late on 3rd January, and Reuters reported that preparations were underway to take the vessel in tow, stern first, to prevent further flooding, and that a hawser would be passed through the starboard fairlead. The American destroyer *John W. Weeks* was standing by to take off Captain Carlsen in the event of a sudden emergency. The raging seas were, however, to thwart repeated attempts to get a towline aboard. By the early hours of 4th January the heavily-listing vessel, now dropping slightly in the bow, had her screw clear of the water and her rudder swinging free. It was a critical situation, which called for all the skill and resourcefulness that those aboard the tug could muster. Captain Carlsen, who was obliged to hang onto his listing, lurching ship for dear life with one hand, was not in a position to haul in a heavy line with the other. Therefore, the only thing to do was to get one of his men aboard. Then, as the *Turmoil* made an approach and the two vessels were almost flung together by the force of the storm, the tug's mate, 27 year old Ken Dancy made a daring and heroic leap aboard the stricken vessel, greeting the surprised captain with the words, 'Captain Carlsen, I presume!' Although Carlsen welcomed his help and his company, he later admitted that the responsibility for this young man's life tended to add to his burden. After a line had been established between the tug and the *Flying Enterprise*, they were able to send food across to them in sea bags. This included sandwiches, roast chicken, still hot, and coffee in a thermos. 'I still remember trying to lift those damn sea bags with my bare hands,' he recalled later. 'They filled with water coming across.'

A message sent from the destroyer *John W. Weeks* at 2.30 pm stated, 'On two latest attempts to rig gear through stern choke, gear parted both times. Mate of tug *Turmoil* managed to get on board over taffrail of steamer *Flying Enterprise*, and is now standing by with Captain Carlsen. Further attempts have been suspended until weather improves. Master of tug *Turmoil* is confident he can get tow rigged if we get a break in weather and will resume efforts day or night. Weather same as last report, except fog closing in and wind increasing to force 7 (moderate gale) at times. *Flying Enterprise* has increased list very slightly but is still buoyant and riding satisfactorily.' Meanwhile, the US destroyer *Willard Keith*, which had been on its way to Plymouth from Bordeaux, was diverted to relieve the destroyer *John W. Weeks*, and the French tug *Abeille No. 25* was heading to the scene to offer assistance to the *Turmoil*, if necessary.

The weather had moderated slightly by the next morning, but the fog was hampering attempts to connect the tow. However, at 9.27 am, there was great elation when they finally achieved success, and the tug proceeded towards Falmouth with the casualty in tow, with Carlsen and Dancy still aboard, escorted by the destroyer *Willard Keith* through moderate seas, with a moderate swell. Meanwhile, back in Falmouth the sole topic of conversation on the waterfront, in pubs, buses and on street corners was the rollicking drama of the *Flying Enterprise*, and her chances of being towed safely to port. But, for the relatives of those aboard the *Turmoil*, it became an increasingly stressful and anxious time.

For a while, things seemed to be going well, with the *Flying Enterprise* riding more easily under tow. She was listing 45° to 50° to port and rolling 70°, while travelling at a speed of about 3½ knots. As darkness fell she represented quite a hazard to shipping, for, although the tug was well illuminated, the *Flying Enterprise* exhibited no lights. So all the vessels in the area were requested to give the convoy a wide berth. On the afternoon of the 6th, when the sea had become slight with a moderate westerly swell and the weather was overcast with some foggy patches, the *Flying Enterprise* was reported to be yawing 40° but riding easily, with no increase in her list. With the barometer remaining steady, there was reason to be optimistic. But at dawn on the 7th, when the wind was described as moderate, the tow started to sheer badly. The wind eased off a bit during the day, and that evening they decided to increase their speed, estimating that they would reach port on the morning of Wednesday, 9th January. Up went the flags and bunting as the folk of Falmouth prepared to give these brave sea-dogs the sort of welcome they would never forget.

At dawn on January 8th, the wind, again described as moderate, blew from the south-south-west and there was a moderate swell. By mid afternoon the weather was deteriorating, impeding the cautious progress of the small convoy, and at 5.45 pm they were forced to heave to. All vessels in the vicinity of lat. 49 26 N, long. 6 10 W were requested to keep well clear. An hour later, it was reported that the vessel, which was still taking in water, was riding lower and rolling heavily, and that she had lost her port lifeboat. However, at 11.20 pm the situation improved and they were underway again. But at 1.30 the following morning there was a serious setback. The towline parted, and she started drifting with the wind. Second Officer Don York of the tug *Turmoil* recalled, 'On the night the tow parted I was on watch and the *Flying Enterprise* was yawing very badly. At 0120 she appeared to be dead astern and quite comfortable. I was quite satisfied with the position of the ship, when suddenly the electric towing gear began to hum. This meant the tow had parted. There was excited shouting up the voice pipe from the engine-room and I immediately called Captain Parker, who was in his cabin, by knocking on the door, and shouted out, "The tow's gone." Parker went to the bridge and I rushed to the aft end of the ship. *Enterprise* was on her own. That was when the panic started. Up to this point I had considered this tow a "piece of cake" to a tug like the *Turmoil*, and not nearly so tricky as many previous salvage operations we had done.' With the vessel rolling heavily, inspection of the cable was impossible, and they had to wait until daylight before an attempt could be made to re-rig the tow.

At 10 am, when they were reported to be 30 miles south of Land's End, the *Turmoil* was attempting to provide shelter for the casualty from wind and weather, while Carlsen and Dancy endeavoured to cut off the main shackle, which had been damaged during the night. The wire had parted in the vicinity of her bow chock. The *Flying Enterprise* was now rolling 80° to port and pitching, and spray was breaking over her main bow. Although there was good visibility and spells of sunshine at the scene of the emergency, the weather was in capricious mood. Winds of 20 knots now veered west-north-west. Rough seas and sudden volleys of sharp, stinging hail knocked the men off their feet and forced efforts to be abandoned for a while. Then, having cleared the shackle, they had to wait for conditions to moderate before resuming operations.

With the wind veering to the west and the casualty being pounded by rough seas, with 20 to 25 ft swells, the *Flying Enterprise* was seen to be riding lower in the water and the deckhouse was awash on the port side. On resuming work, Carlsen and Dancy had a narrow escape from being washed into the sea while they were working at the bow, attempting to re-rig. Lines had been passed to the steamer, but the two men were unable to complete the connection.

That evening a three-way radio conference between Captain Carlsen, the *Turmoil* and the *Willard Keith* determined that Carlsen and Dancy should attempt to lower anchor. *Turmoil* and the destroyer, with a towline strung between them, would endeavour to sweep under the freighter and hook up the hanging anchor. At this crucial time, an encouraging message from Dancy's mother urged him to 'Stick it out, and grit your teeth!' Later that evening, an officer aboard the *Willard*

Keith told Reuters that the *Flying Enterprise* still had a good chance of reaching Falmouth and safety, but that it was very doubtful that they would get there the following day.

At 11.15 pm the Overseas Towage & Salvage Company Limited reported, 'Following telephone message received from Land's End at 10.55 pm: 'Following distress procedure has been arranged by tug *Turmoil* and the ships concerned in the event of it being decided to abandon the casualty: Captain Carlsen and Mr Dancy will fire flares. On sighting this signal the tugs and destroyers in attendance will illuminate the *Flying Enterprise*. At the best opportunity Captain Carlsen and Mr Dancy will jump into the sea, most likely from the stern as conditions may dictate, to be picked up by the nearest vessel. Land's End Radio have the necessary wireless procedure ready to put into operation immediately on being advised to do so by tug *Turmoil*.'

That night the Trinity House vessel *Satellite* put to sea, carrying a breeches buoy, which might prove useful if the vessel, which was now a little lower in the water, should suddenly go down, and at 1.15 am the owners of the tug requested lifeboat assistance. The *Flying Enterprise* was now about 30 miles south of the Lizard, where there was a fresh to moderate gale from the west-north-west and rough seas with 9 ft swells. The tugs *Dexterous*, *Abeille No. 25* and *Turmoil* were standing by on full alert. The captain was still refusing to leave his ship, but a signal from the *Flying Enterprise* and the *Willard Keith* could send them into action at any moment.

When the Lizard lifeboat *Duke of York* was launched at 2.40 am, under the command of coxswain George Mitchell, the Honorary Secretary, Mr F.G. Chapman, who was also aboard, recalled, 'Spray started to fly aboard immediately. It didn't stop coming in every few seconds for 17 hours. The only variation was the occasional arrival of green seas on the deck, which could, and did, knock one across the boat . . . We went on and on, up to the crests and down into the troughs of the 20 ft waves. Not the smooth, regular waves of a ground swell, but steep, irregular fellows that suddenly shot up pinnacles of water to give you a smack as you passed. My wellingtons were full of water, and had been for a long time. Spray which didn't get into my eyes and mouth ran off my face and down my neck and gradually penetrated inside all clothing, lower and lower, until it met the stream soaking upwards from the knees. I realised that this is one of the discomforts lifeboatmen endure and don't talk about . . .' When the lifeboat had been at sea for two hours, the casualty's amended position was received by radio. She was then said to be 34 miles SSE of the Lizard. The coxswain altered course accordingly and, after a hard journey of nearly five and a half hours, at full speed, in a very rough sea, with sheets of spray breaking over her continuously, the *Duke of York* came up with the drifting ship, with the *Turmoil* and the destroyer *Willard Keith* standing by her.

The lifeboat, which had arrived on the scene at 8 am, approached the casualty and proceeded to cruise around her at close quarters for four hours, after which time the *Turmoil* informed her by radio that the captain and Dancy did not intend to leave the ship. It was now noon and, as her fuel was getting low and as the *Flying Enterprise* did not appear to be in imminent danger of sinking, the lifeboat made for her station. However, her return progress was slow and laboured, and one member of the crew, who was knocked off his feet by a wave, narrowly escaped being washed overboard. When darkness fell and they realised that they had little chance of beaching safely at Polpeor in these hazardous conditions, they decided to make for Falmouth. It took nearly eight hours to get there, by which time they were almost out of fuel. They had been at sea for a gruelling 17½ hours, having had no food to sustain them in all that time, apart from a few biscuits, and nothing to drink. Then the news they received on their arrival added disappointment to their experiences of hardship and frustration. When it was known that the Lizard lifeboat needed to refuel, the Cadgwith lifeboat had been alerted, and the *Guide of Dunkirk* was launched to take over her duties. The Falmouth lifeboat *Crawford & Constance Conybeare* also put to sea but, in the event, both were recalled . . .

Not long after the departure of the Lizard lifeboat, it became apparent that the *Flying Enterprise* was doomed, and a message received from the destroyer *Willard Keith*, via the Land's End Radio at 3.09 pm that afternoon, stated, 'Steamer *Flying Enterprise* is going down. We are making efforts to rescue men.' Don York, second officer of the tug *Turmoil*, who was on watch at the time, said shortly afterwards, 'The weather had seriously deteriorated and a westerly gale was blowing with a heavy swell, which washed sea over our decks. *Enterprise* was shipping heavy water along her port side, and appeared to be listing at a more dangerous angle. We were doing out runs closer every time to the *Enterprise* as we were zig-zagging in, watching her condition minute by minute. At 1520 we were close in to the *Enterprise*, when I noticed that the aft hatch covers had been wrenched by the boiling seas and high wind. It was at this time I realised the situation was critical. I called Captain Parker onto the bridge and he said, "It looks as though she's had it now!" Seas were still breaking over her around the damaged hatch cover, and Captain Parker kept the *Turmoil* as close to her as possible. It was shortly after that she took the list that was to mean her end. Until then I had not noticed if Carlsen and Dancy were on deck, since I had been too worried about keeping

Dancy and Carlsen abandon ship

the *Turmoil* as close as possible to the *Enterprise*. Almost immediately after she took her fatal list, I noticed Carlsen and Dancy were huddled to the smoke stack. Captain Parker sent me down to the rails of our ship to assist Carlsen and Dancy aboard when they jumped.

'By this time the *Enterprise* was lying flat on her port side and beginning to prepare for her death plunge, with her bow lifted from the water. Carlsen and Dancy had started to make their way along the smoke stack which was almost awash. We stood by with rescue gear, which we had had rigged for two days, expecting this final sad chapter to become an outstanding epic in sea history! Then came the dramatic jump. Dancy jumped first from the tip of the smoke stack and started striking out towards the *Turmoil*. Carlsen, after a final glance at his slowly sinking ship, also leapt. Dancy tried to see what had happened to Carlsen and a huge wave dropped them close together. By then we were as close to the *Enterprise* as we could safely be.' The *Turmoil* swung her stern into the swell and lowered the Jacob's ladder. Captain Parker had brought his tug as close as remotest limits of safety would allow. The two men were in the water for about nine minutes, before they managed to reach the *Turmoil's* rescue gear. After scrambling up the ladder, they were hauled aboard. Although Captain Carlsen was well nigh exhausted after his heroic ordeal, he immediately expressed his appreciation of their tireless efforts, saying, "Thank you, boys. You have done a good job." Captain Parker later disclosed that he had not taken his clothes off to go to bed from 27th December until 17th January, when he enjoyed a good bath.

At 3.30 pm the French tug *Abeille No. 25* reported, 'The two men are safe on the tug *Turmoil*,' and at 3.43 pm the destroyer *Willard Keith* reported, 'Steamer *Flying Enterprise* is now on her side, 90 per cent under water, but still afloat.' Then the United States Navy Headquarters in London reported that 'the steamer *Flying Enterprise* sank at 4.12 pm GMT today, in position lat. 49 38 N, long. 4 23 W,' and a wireless report from the *Willard Keith* at 4.27 pm stated that the stern of the *Flying Enterprise* was now out of sight.

As the tug *Turmoil*, with Carlsen and Dancy aboard, made for the port of Falmouth, a number of vessels, including the Trinity House vessel *Satellite*, remained in the area, where a vast amount of floating debris constituted a considerable hazard to navigation. Focus was again on the nature of the cargo she was carrying, and a message from Reuters in New York on that day stated, 'The following is the cargo the steamer *Flying Enterprise* was carrying when she sank today, as reported at a Coastguard investigation into the sinking: 1,271 tons of pig-iron, 890 tons of African coffee, 55 tons of graphite, 82 tons of bone meal, 800 bales of peat moss, 65 bird cages, five tons of columbite ore, 260 bags of grass seed, 25 barrels of onions, some steel vans loaded with carpets, some barrels of aluminium chloride, some furniture, a number of bales of jute bagging and a number of bales of animal hair from India. The coffee was picked up at Rotterdam.' The master of the Norwegian tanker *Westfal Larsen* placed on record that he had pumped 500 tons of oil overboard and had a lifeboat wrecked while going to the assistance of the *Flying Enterprise*, and the master of the British motor vessel *Sherborne* stated that he had lost a ship's lifeboat in the course of the difficult rescue operation.

Over the course of the next few days substantial quantities of wreckage were cast up on the shores of the Channel Islands and on the French coast. On 19th January it was reported from Guernsey, 'A good deal of flotsam, consisting of mail bags, cases containing personal belongings, large numbers of candles and a quantity of timber, believed to be from steamer *Flying Enterprise*, is being washed ashore on the west coast here. Up to now, most of this flotsam has been collected up by local inhabitants.' Three days later parcels of books, tins of Christmas pudding, packages of chocolates and half a lifebelt marked 'FLYING EN' up to the broken section, were recovered on the north-east coast of Jersey, and other items, including a mahogany hatch cover and a cabin door, appeared on the shores of Iles Chausey, near Granville.

Back in Falmouth, excitement had reached fever pitch and the streets were gaily decorated with welcoming flags and bunting, representing all nationalities. Various notable people, including high-ranking American officers, a representative of the Danish ambassador and a whole host of newspaper reporters from all over the world, were in Falmouth, and visitors keen to witness the historic end to the drama flocked in by the bus and train load. Noisy aeroplanes droned continually overhead, but all eyes were focused expectantly on the greeny-blue waters of Falmouth Bay, flecked with white horses. At about eight o'clock that evening, the sturdy tug *Turmoil* ploughed her triumphant way homewards through the stormy waters and entered the mouth of Falmouth harbour, which was illuminated by an array of cars' head-lights from the headlands of Pendennis and St Mawes. There arose a rousing cacaphony of sound as cheers rang out and vessels in the harbour saluted her safe return on their sirens. Crowds of people who had braved the cold and blustering wind and rain in the hopes of catching a glimpse of the heroes were disappointed, for they kept a very low profile.

Forty years on, Steve Pellow, who worked at the office of G.C. Fox & Co., the long-established shipping agents in Falmouth, still recalled that night vividly. 'In those days, prior to Telex and Fax machines, I had to sleep in the office, for practically all the emergency calls came during the night. On that particular night I had no chance of going to bed at all. I spent the whole night with a duffle coat on over my pyjamas, answering the phone in the main office. I could have made a fortune that night, because the world's press was in and around Falmouth, and they were offering quite large sums of money for the exclusive use of a telephone, particularly the American press, who were lined up outside this office, knocking on the door, hoping that I would admit them. And there was I, busy on one telephone, with about four or five telephones around me, not being used. I felt tempted to let them in, but I resisted the temptation. Anyway, one of the funny things that happened during the night was that about 4 or 5 am I had a telephone call from one of the superintendents of the owners of the *Flying Enterprise*, Isbrandtsen. They had suddenly realised that Captain Carlsen, who was due to have a civic reception at ten o'clock that morning, didn't have a uniform to wear, and could we do anything about it? So I said I would get hold of a tailor to come down to the ship as early as possible. I think at that time he was on board the American destroyer which berthed in the docks that night. There used to be a Geoff Phillips, who had a tailor's shop next door to the office, so I dug him out of bed about 5 or 6 am, and asked him if he would go down to the American destroyer, see Captain Carlsen, measure him and get him fixed up in a uniform by 10 am, which he did.'

On 11th January, Captain Carlsen and Ken Dancy stepped ashore to a true hero's welcome, amidst a blaze of publicity, and a full-scale civic reception awaited them on a platform on the pier. Captain Carlsen's heroism had been recognised by King Frederick of Denmark, who bestowed upon him the honour of becoming a Knight of the Order of Danneborg, and the Danish Ambassador was here to make the decoration. The Continental *Daily Mail* sent a 200 lb crate of gifts for him. Honours abounded. The following day he was awarded the Lloyd's Silver Medal in London, for his brave actions had meant that no other shipping company could claim the *Flying Enterprise* for salvage. His heroism also won him a special Merchant Marine Distinguished Service Award from the United States Congress, and other maritime medals were awarded to him by Belgium, France and Morocco. The hero of the sea went on to experience a full scale ticker-tape welcome in New York. Then there was another boisterous reception in his home town of Woodbridge, New Jersey, where he lived with his Danish-born wife, Agnes, and his two daughters.

Fortunately, some other heroes of this drama also received recognition and Admiral E.L.S. King wrote, 'I should be glad if you would convey to the crew of the Lizard lifeboat my congratulations on the excellent service rendered in connection with the *Flying Enterprise*.

Knowing as I do the difficulty of locating a ship under such weather conditions, the Coxswain is especially to be congratulated on his navigation. It was a rough and unpleasant trip for all hands . . .' Further to this humanitarian theme, a new Dutch lifeboat, which was commissioned at the newly opened lifeboat station at Noordwijk aan Zee on 13th July 1952, was named the *Kurt Carlsen*, and the indefatigable captain travelled there specially to unveil the teak motor lifeboat in her smart blue and white livery.

Captain Carlsen gave a press conference in Falmouth soon after his arrival and, in response to being offered £30,000 for his exclusive story, had retorted, 'Why should I make money out of a disaster, when I was being paid to do my duty as a master mariner?'

During the investigations which followed, Dutch sources reported that the crew of the *Flying Enterprise* said that they could not understand why they were not allowed to make for the nearest port when the trouble first started. But when they asked the captain about this, Carlsen had said that he was awaiting orders from the ship's owners in New York. The crew also criticised the fact that he waited 28½ hours before sending out the first SOS. During that time, no one, apart from Isbrandtsen, knew that the vessel's hull had split.

Over the next few decades, speculation continued in regard to the true nature of the cargo. The Italian salvage company Sorima Societa Ricuperi Marittimi, which carried out operations on the wreck in June and July 1953, when she was lying in 80 metres of water, recovered large numbers of typewriters, toys, several crates of Volkswagen motor spares, over 600 tons of pig-iron, and about £110,000 worth of sterling and dollar banknotes. These were taken ashore in Ostend. Dutch sources reported that Jacob Isbrandtsen, President of the Isbrandtsen Shipping Company, was said to be very surprised by the find, as it was not on the ship's manifesto. Rumour had it that these were secret German funds, and this did not seem too strange, as there happened to be some Volkswagens on board, bound for South America. They put a salvage value of Fr. 750,000 on it. Captain Carlsen, who happened to be in Singapore at the time, told the press that he did not believe the rumours in regard to the banknotes and pointed out, 'If that money had been on board, it would have been easy to get it off before the ship sank.'

This statement had been regarded as plausible, as several days had elapsed between the first SOS and the time the ship went down. Furthermore, Captain Carlsen suggested that the banknotes could have been removed from some unknown ship. This suggestion was dismissed by the salvors, who insisted that the money definitely came off the wreck of the *Flying Enterprise*. Photographs were taken of the banknotes being dried out in the Bank of Brussels; they became much-prized trophies, framed and placed on the walls of prestigious offices. But, even after this revelation, there was a widespread feeling that all had not yet been revealed in this bizarre and swashbuckling epic of the sea.

When the American nuclear submarine *Nautilus* made its first test dive in January 1955, strong rumours filtered through from New York that the *Flying Enterprise* had been carrying a priceless cargo of zirconium, imperative in the building of the first nuclear-powered submarine, and that the loss of this cargo had been a big setback for the United States Navy, for it had delayed the completion of the project by many months. In 1951 there was only one factory in the free world, based in Hamburg, where they could separate zirconium from hafnium, and the raw materials of these two metals were transported from Brazil to Hamburg. However, a spokesman for Isbrandtsen issued a prompt statement in regard to such an outrageous suggestion, saying that as far as they knew, no precious metal bound for the *Nautilus* had ever been on board the *Flying Enterprise*; while the authorities in Washington denied all knowledge of it.

In 1987, Miss Kate Dinn, curator of the Falmouth Art Gallery, decided to mark the 35th anniversary of this great sea drama by staging a commemorative exhibition, hoping to bring the two seafarers together again, to be honoured once more by the port and its people. She discovered that Captain Carlsen was still living in the United States and that Ken Dancy was living in Holland. There was great disappointment when it was disclosed that Captain Carlsen was suffering from Parkinson's disease, and was not well enough to attend. Sadly, this bold hero of the sea, who had become a living legend, died two years later at the age of 75. It was almost a case of taking his remarkable secret to the grave, but in a telephone conversation with Miss Dinn in December 1986, he told her that the *Flying Enterprise* was indeed carrying zirconium in sealed containers, thereby confirming the most lurid of speculations. However, the final irony of it all was that he had been unaware of this, until being enlightened by a Russian informer shortly afterwards, when he was as surprised as anyone. As for an explanation as to why he behaved in the way he did, he said it was the duty of any captain to remain with his ship.

In 1994, some of the old watermen of Falmouth, who had been giving in-port assistance to the Italian salvage company after the *Flying Enterprise* drama, told me, 'There was things we 'eard, as we couldn't talk about . . . Things what the divers 'ad found aboard 'er and that . . . There's some as wanted 'er to go down – on account o' the cargo she were carryin'!'

12

They Called the Baby 'Harlyn'

◆

When the barque *Viking* of Sunderland left the port of Cardiff on the last day of March 1872, bound for Plymouth with a large cargo of coal, Captain Gentles and his crew had no reason to believe that this trip would be different from any other, for they were familiar with this run and had faith in their trusty barque. Indeed, the master had brought his wife and young baby aboard to share the voyage with him, for this was a seafaring family, where sons, who often found their sea legs before they could walk on land, were proud to follow fathers in a lifetime of service at sea. If this was to be in the nature of an initiation, what an initiation it turned out to be!

There was a gentle breeze as they sailed out of Cardiff on the Saturday, but as they were passing Lundy Island the wind veered to the north-west, and then north-north-west, strengthening to gale and severe gale force, whipping up ferocious seas along the Cornish coast. Skippers who had not been able to reach shelter in a port of refuge, which were few and far between along these formidable shores, knew that riding out the storm at sea was safer in such conditions. The *Viking*, however, found herself being driven too close to the shore and was unable to rectify the situation.

The West Briton of 4th April reported:

'On Monday night she passed Lundy Island, and the wind veering round to the north-west and blowing strongly, the captain decided upon running for Padstow. He failed to make that harbour, however, and he then made for Perleze or Harlyn Bay, in which he brought his vessel to anchor at 2 o'clock on Monday afternoon. Shortly after anchoring, the rudder, owing to the stormy sea, got unshipped and knocked a hole in the vessel's stern, and finding that the ship was making water, the captain slipped the anchor and beached her.'

The Trevose Head and Crugmeer rocket brigades, who had noticed that she was in difficulties and followed her plight, waited until she struck before attempting to fire a line to her by rocket. It was a triumph in the face of wind and weather when they succeeded in getting a line to the casualty, but high hopes were cruelly dashed when the flapping line became entangled in the rocks. In the stress of the moment, three impetuous crewmen plunged into the heaving surf, and miraculously made it safely to the shore.

While this was happening, the Padstow lifeboat crew, who had been kept in touch with events, prepared for a service which was to stay vividly in their minds for the rest of their days. The local seafaring fraternity knew all too well the perils of the sea when the wind was in that quarter. The time when wise fishermen would choose to stay at home, and cautious captains sought safe havens, was the very time that gallant lifeboat crews, mainly made up of fishermen, usually put to sea and faced the full fury of the elements in their everyday environment.

When they knew that the distressed vessel was running into Harlyn Bay, the lifeboat crew sprinted over the cliffs to Hawker's Cove to launch their lifeboat *Albert Edward*. They took her upstream to Padstow, to be placed on a carriage and hauled overland by a team of ten horses, for it would have been impossible to reach them by sea in these conditions. At times like this the whole population turned out to lend a hand. When the heavy lifeboat was safely on its carriage, the team started off along the quay, and officials went ahead to clear the way as the horses took the steep hill at a gallop. There were many willing helpers to push and pull and generally assist along the way.

When they reached Harlyn Bay just after five o'clock, they found the stricken vessel some distance from the shore, which meant that they would have to launch into the teeth of the gale. We can only marvel at the courage and endurance of these early lifeboatmen. Having already expended a great deal of energy in getting the lifeboat thus far, they had to manoeuvre her through soft sands and launch into shallow waters through the heavy surf. Launching in this way was a highly dangerous business, fraught with the dangers of capsizing and being swept away in the undertow. When they managed to get the *Albert Edward* afloat, they were promptly swamped by an enormous wave, which broke right over them, but, nothing daunted they strained at the oars and heaved away with all their strength, until they eventually reached the distressed vessel. Crewman Andrew Crennel recalled many years later, 'I was pulling the lee-bow oar, and when we got out to the *Viking* I had the job of keeping the *Albert Edward*'s bow up to the wind and sea. The breakers were sweeping right over the vessel, and pouring down over us.' When they succeeded in getting a line aboard her, able seaman

George Thomas plays his part

George Thomas brought the captain's small baby across in a warm, red muffler, carefully lashed around him, and landed on the whaleback, to allow the bowman to cut away the muffler and take hold of the baby. But in doing so he tragically forfeited his own life, for he was swept away by a huge sea before he was able to jump into the lifeboat. Shocked and appalled as they were, the operation to save the captain, his wife and the rest of the crew had to go ahead. 'The mother of the baby didn't come down the line, but jumped overboard with a line her husband had fastened around her,' recalled Andrew Crennel. 'In the water we had a momentary glimpse of a white face, a pair of glazed eyes, and a mass of black hair and skirts floating about – then we had her aboard.'

The lifeboatmen proceeded to take off the remainder of the crew one by one. However, the elderly cook refused to come down the line. He lashed himself to a ladder and jumped into the angry waters, and, after being tossed around by the waves, he was yielded up unconscious on the shore and revived by artificial respiration. The captain was the last to leave his ship, and all were safely landed by early evening, then taken to Harlyn House, where Mr Hellyer, the proprietor, provided them with dry clothes, refreshments and warm beds.

Shortly afterwards the folk of Padstow were pleased to learn that the Duke of Edinburgh made mention of these noble deeds in his speech at the annual meeting of the RNLI, and further prestige came to Padstow when the coxswain, William Corkhill, and the second coxswain, Samuel Bate, were awarded Silver Medals for the rescue of seven persons from the barque *Viking*, wrecked in Harlyn Bay on 2nd April 1872. The angelic face of that baby remained with those lifeboatmen in their waking hours, and in their dreams, and the tale was often repeated around the firesides on long winters' evenings. 'They called the baby "Harlyn", in honour of the heroic rescue, and with thanks for their safe deliverance,' the lifeboatmen said, 'and when he grew up he became the captain of a liner that sailed the Seven Seas.' That would have made the perfect ending to the story, but some thought it was wishful thinking.

A century later, when the author was yarning with the crew aboard an Australian-bound ocean liner, a seasoned seafarer told of his early days at sea, when he served under an eccentric old captain who claimed to have been saved from a shipwreck off Padstow when he was a baby. 'A likely story!' everyone chuckled. Old Wiggie's far-seeing eyes glowed beneath his bushy brows as he re-lit his pipe. 'The old boy swore it was true,' he said. 'But I ask you, who'd ever believe a tale as far fetched as that?'

13

Fracas in St Ives

◆

Captain Thomas Harris reckoned it was his lucky day when the lugger *Mary Ellen* of Shoreham fell in with a deserted wreck ten miles north-west of St Ives as he made his way out to the fishing grounds in 'May month' 1869. The trouble was, so did a lot of other people.

Other fishing vessels were quick to offer assistance, but the salvors knew that there was going to be trouble as soon as they spotted the splendid steam-tugs *Bride* and *Warrior* approaching. They suspected certain tug-boat captains and a variety of other officials of being in league with Harvey's of Hayle, for they had an annoying habit of siphoning off trade from St Ives. This had given rise to a certain bitterness, and the men of St Ives had retaliated when it came to them trying the same trick with a Brazilian coffee ship and the Spanish barque *Maria Clotilde* a few months earlier. Now they kept an eye out as the tugs circled the derelict, transferred a boatload of men from the *Bride* to the *Warrior* and came alongside the wreck. A Customs House official was in the boat and, although the fishermen declined offers of assistance, those in the boat insisted on taking the ship in tow. Without more ado the intruders set about cutting her keel in preparation for doing so – whatever their objections. But the brawny fishermen had ways of warding off their rivals, who were eventually obliged to retreat to their sophisticated tugs. As the derelict appeared off St Ives Head in the tow of 18 fishing luggers, one Mr James Henry Redfern rushed off to send a telegram to the Collector of Customs at Hayle.

Towing her in with drifters was no mean achievement, for the up-turned vessel was over 90 ft in length. What a triumphal spectacle they must have created as they proudly bore their splendid prize into their home port of St Ives, for she was nearly new, coppered and of about 270 tons burthen. A chest, some soggy clothes and documents washed out of the round house were the sole and eerie reminders of her ill-fated crew, and it was soon established that she was the Norwegian brig *Rypen*, which had recently left Ibrail and Queenstown for Dover. Her salvage value was estimated at around £500 and, in the course of the next few days, the *Rypen* was to reveal rather more than was comfortable about human nature, and create more excitement in St Ives, than PC James Bennetts had encountered in all his eleven years of being a policeman there.

The removal of the wreck had been a maritime service in its own right, for it had constituted a navigational hazard to shipping. In pursuing this as a salvage operation, the fishermen were well aware of possible entanglements by red tape and went out of their way to follow the correct procedure. So they anchored the ship about a quarter of a mile from the new pier, to await orders from the Harbour Master and reported the situation to the Receiver of Wreck.

Captain Thomas Richards, the Harbour Master, whose responsibility it was to issue instructions for the safety of vessels entering the port, told them to bring her in as far as they could and pointed out that part of the harbour where vessels should lie. So they hove her closer to the Old Pier Head, and shipwright William Williams was called upon to bore a large hole in her keel to take a bolt to fasten her securely to the pier-head warp. Shipkeepers were placed on board and the next day salvors started to remove the rigging and other materials, which were duly delivered to the Receiver of Wreck. When the vessel was righted, the shipwright bored holes to release the pent-up water and prevent her from straining under the pressure. Then she was made tight and they set about excavating a dock in the sand, so that she could be floated in on the next tide. All this was planned and set in motion by those well-versed in maritime skills, and the story would have ended here, had it not been for the untimely interference of some who were not.

Mr William Henry Holmes, Collector of Customs at Hayle and Receiver of Wreck for an area extending from Gurnard's Head to Chapel Angather in Perranzabuloe, having been alerted by his deputy at St Ives, Mr Redfern, who was also a coastguard officer, gave instructions to the chief salvor that the vessel should not be brought into shallow water if it could possibly be avoided, and that she should be swept to ascertain whether any masts, anchors or other impediments might hamper attempts to right her. He also informed them that the Chief Officer of the Coastguard and the Deputy Receiver of Wreck would supply gear and offer assistance. When he left Hayle, the derelict had been in the roadstead, not in the harbour and he left her in the charge of the chief salvor. Next day he went to St Ives and examined some seamen's effects, including letters and papers which had been washed ashore and had been placed in the possession of the Receiver. The wreck was in the charge of the chief salvor, supervised by the Deputy Receiver, and Chief Officer to the Coastguard. At that time the wreck was situated in line with the point at the west of Hayle Bar and the new pier-head. But it was fast becoming a case of too many chiefs and too many Indians.

Mr Holmes, who was of a determined and somewhat officious disposition, may have felt he was not so much in command of the situation as he might have wished. So he returned the following day with one of his old associates of Hayle, Mr William John Rawlings, a merchant, who had fingers in a number of pies and fulfilled the role of Vice-Consul for Norway and Sweden. Mr Rawlings had been in touch with the Consul General of Norway in London, to ascertain what steps he should take, and at first he was reluctant to carry out an inspection of the vessel, as he did not think this was within his province. Mr Holmes, however, had drawn his attention to Minute 50 in his Consular Instructions, and convinced him that he was duty-bound to do so, on account of there being no master or mate in charge of the derelict.

When they arrived, about 90 men were working at the site, like noisy bees around a honey pot. The appearance of these affected, nosy officials did not go down too well, particularly as they were known to be from Hayle, and suspected by some of having taken backhanders from Harvey's. The two men spoke to the chief salvor and other officials and were assured that this was the best place for the wreck to be, provided that it was properly moored. So they made a show of checking this and that, and strutting about looking important. At about midday Mr Holmes, Mr Rawlings, Mr Redfern and Mr Martin, Chief Officer of the Coastguard at St Ives, went on board to inspect the ship and Mr Rawlings went into the hold and searched in vain for the word 'Norakeindon', which, according to Norwegian law ought to have been there.

'Would you say that this ship is safely moored?' Mr Rawlings asked Captain Harris, the chief salvor, and his second-in-command, and on being told that she was, ventured to enquire whether there was sufficient chain to keep her and other equally fatuous questions to put to men of the sea. After dealing patiently with a repetitive barrage from them all, Captain Harris expressed concern about the escalating number of people attaching themselves to this operation, eroding salvage money and expenses. 'Sixty of the ninety people 'ere should be paid as assistants, not salvors,' he said, and he agreed to remain on board until his claim was settled. It was arranged that two customs men should also remain on the vessel, and that the present shipkeepers should be discharged. There were sighs of relief when the officials wobbled their way down the gang plank. But the worst was still to come.

As they were leaving the vessel, they noticed some men digging in the sand at her bow. 'What is going on here?' demanded Mr Holmes.

'We're excavatin' a dock, they explained, 'so that we can get 'er further in on the next 'igh tide.' 'But I expressly said that she was not to be taken any further in!' exclaimed Mr Holmes beginning to get rattled. 'That's because they want to take 'er out easy, so as ter get 'er round to 'Ayle,' whispered someone. 'Tell them to stop!' said Mr Holmes to Mr Redfern, rapidly losing his grip on the situation. 'We're doin' this on the direction of the 'Arbour Master, 'oo 'as overall responsibility for the safety of all vessels in the 'arbour. If we leave 'er 'ere an' she do forge a'ead on the tide, she'll break 'er back an' be a danger to other shippin',' reasoned one of the salvors.

But common sense was not to be the order of the day. Mr Holmes was hopping around in a rage, and putting the onus on his deputy. 'I'm ordering you to stop digging!' shouted Mr Redfern in his sternest tones. 'You 'ave nothing to do with this ship at all. She belongs to us!' retorted one of the diggers, whereupon every man picked up his shovel and carried on digging. If the salvors were affronted by such highhandedness, the pompous, self-appointed officials did not like being put in their places in this way.

Some of the bystanders were beginning to get a bit excited by this time and one of them gave Mr Redfern a nudge, to encourage him to leave the scene. 'Who pushed me?' he cried in agitation, and became more annoyed as the people looked innocently about them and no one volunteered any information. 'Somebody gave me a push in the back!' he complained to Mr Holmes, who then added fuel to the flames by demanding to know who was responsible and became more and more heated at the realisation that the crowd was hostile towards them. 'I will give a reward of £5 to anyone who will name the person who pushed Mr Redfern!' he shouted at the top of his voice, but nobody was willing to give any information about the offender. This was a situation relished by the diggers of the dock, who threw in a few cryptic comments, and Mr Holmes, white with anger, muttered, 'I'd like to shoot the lot of 'em!' (or words to that effect).

Just before he left the scene, Mr Holmes was heard to say above the general clamour that he would leave the vessel in Mr Redfern's charge and would hold him responsible for the safety of the ship. 'If these men should attempt to move the vessel, you will resist, by force if necessary.' Then, possibly realising that this might be a slightly unequal contest, he instructed another of his henchmen to assist Mr Redfern, adding the bizarre rider, 'And if there is a need to employ force, I should not care if half a dozen got shot in the process!'

Back at the Custom House, Mr John Tremearne, the Lloyd's agent, asked Mr Holmes what orders he had given concerning the *Rypen*, and said that he and some of the salvors who had come to see him thought that she ought to be brought further in. However, as Mr Holmes failed to climb down in the face of expert opinion, he thought it might be diplomatic to suggest that, as there was a dispute, the matter should be put in the hands of an independent, licensed pilot, who would have written authority and would therefore carry any responsibility for moving the ship. As this brought howls of dissension from the salvors, he tried to soften that by saying that they could choose their own pilot, as long as he was licensed. 'But why do we 'ave to 'ave a pilot?' they asked. ''E 'll need ter be aboard at ev'ry tide, an' will cost a tidy packet. We could do the job as well as any pilot.' Thinking that their objections might be a matter of finance rather than injured pride, Mr Tremearne assured them that it would not affect their salvage money. So, hoping that he had satisfied everyone, he sat down and composed a letter, which he addressed to 'A Licensed Pilot' and handed to Mr Redfern to deliver to the first available pilot. Then Mr Holmes and Mr Rawlings adjourned to an hotel, hoping that things would quieten down.

It was now the thirteenth day of May and, as luck would have it, John Andrews was the unsuspecting pilot who received the request to take charge of the *Rypen*, to judge where she ought to be placed and see her properly moored. But as he attempted to board the vessel by the chain plates, Richard Giles, a salvor, suddenly loomed up and barred his way, saying that they were not going to allow him on board. There was laughter in the court room a few days later when Mr Giles told the Board of Trade Inquiry, ''E wen' away ashore, very quiet.'

Later that afternoon Mr Redfern, Captain Harris and Mr Charles Martin, the Chief Officer of the Coastguard at St Ives, informed Mr Holmes that a group of men had prevented the pilot from going on board the *Rypen*, and he responded by thumping his fist on the table and declaring, 'Oh, they did, did they? I'm not standing for that. If that is the case I will go down to the ship and put a pilot aboard myself!' He disappeared in the direction of the waterfront, while Captain Harris went in search of Mr Rawlings, who had just enjoyed a good meal at the hotel.

Mr Holmes stomped off down to the waterfront, where he came upon a crowd of four or five hundred people surrounding the vessel. They were well behaved, and allowed him to make his way through without hindrance. When he reached the bow, he saw a tackle fastened there, and about 40 men busily working on it. Mr Holmes ordered them to stop work, but they steadfastly refused to do so, 'I hold you responsible for any damage that might befall this ship,' he declared, and directed Mr Redfern, Mr Rawlings, Mr Martin and John Dewstone, commissioned boatman of the Coastguard at St Ives, to back him up in collecting names of the offenders. This did not go down very well with the crowd, who started to edge them towards the water. Some bold individuals demanded that Mr Holmes and his associates leave the beach before things got any worse. 'I'm not going until I've been given at least two names,' he retorted. 'That man is called Veal,' shouted Mr Redfern, pointing at one of the salvors. 'Veal?' scowled Mr Holmes. 'What Veal?' 'My name is John Veal, Junior,' said that gentleman obligingly, taking off his hat with a flourish and waving it in the air. Then, turning to his mates, he exhorted them to carry on with the digging.

The crowd grew noisier and more excited as the unpopular officials attempted to procure more names. Sand was being flung around, and some men made cheeky faces or threatening gestures, calling out comments such as 'Scat their brains in!' and ''Eave 'em in the say!' But the sounds escalated to crescendo pitch, described at the time as being like 'ten thousand screaming cats', after Mr Holmes was heard to say to Mr Martin, 'This is a riot. We must get arms to protect us, and if they persist in digging the dock, shoot half a dozen of them, and I will take the consequences.' Excited folk went running round the streets, crying 'They are going to fire on the people!' or 'They're going to shoot the salvors!' And everyone came rushing down to the shore.

Mr Martin passed on the order to Mr Dewstone, and when he returned, he handed pistols to Mr Holmes and Mr Martin. Mr Holmes then placed a cartridge in the pistol, rammed it down, capped and cocked it, aiming at salvor Edward Mason's head at point blank range. 'I'll fire!' he threatened. To which Ned Mason coolly responded, 'If you shoot, don't miss!' At that moment, and in the nick of time, William Williams, the shipbuilder, leapt from the crowd, thrust Mr Holmes's pistol-aiming arm high above his head, grabbed his coat collar, and, glaring eyeball to eyeball, demanded whether he could answer for the consequences. 'But this is a riot,' came the pathetic reply. 'A riot? If it is a riot, it is a riot of *your* making. It is disgraceful. The very idea of bringing firearms into an excited crowd. You had better leave here immediately.' 'I will, if you will let me,' gasped the trembling bully, and Mr Williams instructed the angry people to clear a way and let him pass. Then he rushed from the scene, darting in and out of the water and dodging among the vessels.

While this was going on, Mr Rawlings, whom some suspected had taken a little too much wine with his dinner, was staggering around and falling over piles of the newly-dug sand. 'Look out! He has firearms, he has firearms!' cried someone, and others took up the theme, pushing him around and pulling out his pockets. 'Nonsense,' he said, trying to resist being pushed into the water. Then someone placed an arm through his, and the crowd kept back. 'It is very unmanly of fifty men to throw themselves on one man, who has no means of defence,' he

'If you shoot, don't miss!'

said. 'If there were one real man amongst the lot of you, he would come to my side and defend me.' Several men stepped forward, then Mr Williams asked him to accompany him from the scene. 'I won't. I am not afraid of any man,' he declared. So Mr Redfern grabbed him and led him, protesting, from the shore. After this the crowd lost interest and started drifting away, and the salvors carried on with their digging. If Mr Rawlings had been a wise man, he would have left it at that. As it was, he tried to summon the arm of the law, but PC Bennetts did not want to know. So he tried to enlist the aid of the Mayor, but Mr Jennings told him that if he was in trouble, he ought to watch the company he kept, acquainted him with a few home truths about the men of Hayle and sent him packing with a flea in his ear.

When it came to the Board of Trade Inquiry, the fearless Mr Rawlings was reluctant to put in an appearance, unless he had adequate protection from the townsfolk of St Ives, and the mayor said he resented that slur on their character. He felt aggrieved, and complained about his treatment at St Ives to the Swedish Ambassador, who drew it to the attention of the Foreign Secretary, who handed it over to the Home Secretary, who forwarded it to the magistrates at St Ives. But potential witnesses denied all knowledge of the charges. When it came to the court case, in which Ned Mason summoned Mr Holmes for assault, Mr Dewstone, who had been subpoenaed that morning, took to his heels and had to be tracked down and brought back by force.

After the three day Inquiry, which had its light-hearted moments, it was acknowledged that the inhabitants of St Ives resented the loss of their Custom House and much of their maritime trade to Hayle, and could get very excited when roused. Mr Tresidder, Clerk to the Harbour Commissioners, pointed out that by the St Ives Harbour Act, 1853, St Ives Order, 1862, and the General Pier Harbour Act Incorporated, 1847, the Harbour Master had power to regulate, moor, place or remove any vessel within the limit of the harbour. At the request of the Chairman, the mayor summed it up by saying that it struck him that the whole of the matter had arisen from an interference with the ordinary duties of an acknowledged authority. His conclusion was that had not Mr Holmes and Mr Redfern been so hasty about the work, and had they allowed Captain Richards's instructions to have been carried out, the whole of the unhappy affray would have been prevented.

When it came to defending Mr Holmes against Ned Mason's charge of assault, the Board of Trade procured themselves a very competent lawyer in Mr Cumberland, who, subscribing to the philosophy that the best means of defence is attack, said that it was very regrettable that this charge had come before the bench. He did not like to say that it had been brought vindictively, but that was what it looked like. He tried to convince them that any derelict property was the property of the Crown, and was hissed at when he put forward the view that the alleged assault took place when there was an illegal assemblage, adding that no one in the court thought that Mr Holmes intended to shoot Mr Mason.

Mr Edmonds, representing Mason, said he had hoped that an admission would have been made by Holmes and that it was a most aggravated assault. He should have acted in a dignified manner, as a representative of his office, and set a good example. As it was he took advantage of his power to commit the assault. He asked the Bench to consider the position of authority that Holmes held in the port, and inflict the highest penalty. But, in the event, the magistrates found him guilty and fined him 5 shillings, plus costs. They considered that the defendant had only himself to blame, and that the object of imposing this nominal fine was to acknowledge that a legal offence had been committed, rather than inflict a punishment.

This liberal approach, which must have stuck in the gullets of the fair-minded folk of St Ives, was eagerly seized on by the Board of Trade, who paid the fine and costs of £4 0s 6d, and claimed it to be tantamount to an acquittal.

14

Fire Down Below!

◆

It was in the month of February in the year of 1825 that the East India Company's ship *Kent* rounded North Foreland and bounced gaily down the English Channel, bound for Bengal and China. This fine vessel of 1,400 tons burthen, commanded by Captain Henry Cobb, had a crew of 145 and was carrying 364 officers and men of the 31st Regiment, their ladies, wives and children, as well as 19 private passengers. There had been scenes of great emotion before the ship sailed, and one of the soldier's wives, whose pleas to accompany her beloved husband on the voyage to India had fallen on deaf ears, had managed to sneak aboard as a stowaway. But little did those aboard this trusty bark realise that this was not so much a floating hotel; more of a lethal, floating fire cracker, just waiting to explode. For in the hold they were carrying 140 tons of ammunition!

If the overcrowded accommodation was a trifle uncomfortable and a few of the passengers felt a little queasy, it was comparatively plain sailing as the barque cleared Dover, Wight, Portland, Plymouth, the Dodman, the Lizard and the Isles of Scilly, and many a tear was shed as she altered course and headed southwards and these much-loved shores disappeared from view. Would they ever set eyes on dear old England again? Seasickness and the first painful pangs of homesickness were trifling in comparison with the incredible experiences which awaited them.

The south-westerly breeze freshened and increased to gale force as they entered the Bay of Biscay and the sturdy, heavily-laden barque battled on, with the wind on her bow quarter, pitching and tossing, screwing and rolling through the turbulent waters and rhythmic bands of heaving swell on that first mad day of March. In a situation like this it was a case of riding out the storm, and the dangers resulting from a shifting cargo upsetting the trim of the ship were more serious than the actual onslaught of wind and wave. Paradoxically, all might have been well, had not the diligent third mate and two of the crew gone below with a lighted lanthorn to check that everything was fast. They noticed that a cask of spirits had come adrift and, during their attempts to make it secure, the inevitable happened. The ship gave an unexpected, violent lurch, the officer stumbled and lost hold of the lanthorn, the cask dislodged and got stove-in, and its highly volatile contents leaked out. Almost immediately a searing shaft of flame shot from the lanthorn, ignited the cask and leapt madly all around. The prospect of fire at sea has always been the dread of every mariner, let alone these, who knew that they were isolated in a stormy ocean, aboard a floating time-bomb. It was a fundamental situation which was to test the true nature of everyone involved, or as the poet put it:

> 'Then rose from sea to sky the wild farewell!
> Then shrieked the timid and stood still the brave.'

Smoke began to appear from the hatchway as Captain Cobb and his officers gave orders to the seamen and soldiers to man the pumps, fetch buckets of water, saturate hammocks and sails to dampen the flames, and isolate the seat of the fire by surrounding it with casks of water. Initially, they had hopes of containing the fire and did not wish the women and children to become alarmed and panic, so they kept the whole operation as low-profile as possible. But, despite their valiant efforts, growing volumes of black, noxious smoke began to emerge from the four hatchways and billow all over the ship, much to the consternation of the passengers who were in the saloons or slumped seasick in their bunks and around the decks.

By now it was obvious that there was little hope of preserving the vessel, and there was an increasing risk that they would all be blown sky-high when the rapid flames licked through to the explosive cargo. The decisive captain, who seemed to gain strength and courage as the emergency grew more acute, gave orders for the lower decks to be scuttled, the combing of the hatches to be cut and the lower ports to be opened. When all this was accomplished the sea rushed in with tremendous force, carrying away large chests, bulkheads and other things in its formidable path as it surged into the hold. Sadly, some of the passengers who had been sick and others who had been unable to reach the upper deck were suffocated in the course of this overall survival strategy. For a time this immense volume of water had the desired effect of checking the fury of the flames. But if the risk of being blown to kingdom-come by gunpowder had diminished, the danger of drowning from a sinking ship had increased. The vessel became water-logged and took on the feel of a ship about to settle before disappearing beneath the waves for ever.

While this was happening, hundreds of passengers, including those who had been stricken with seasickness in their cabins, had been forced up on deck by the suffocating smoke, without having had the opportunity to grab warm clothing. Many, still in their night attire, were making frantic attempts to find members of their families amidst all the confusion. As some rushed around in a wild spurt of energy, borne of blind panic, others became rooted to the spot, in a silent state of shock. Those who calmly knelt and prayed and put their faith in the Lord were an inspiration to others and a comfort to the distressed children, who were told to be mindful of their religious teaching. But, despite all this, some of the little ones in the saloon cabins at the sides of the deck continued to play with their toys, apparently oblivious of all the dangers which surrounded them. Some of the sailors, who strove so valiantly to carry out the captain's orders, wondered whether they would ever set eyes on their loved ones again, for it seemed that this would be their last voyage – on a doomed ship, soon to disappear beneath the cruel waves. For who could know of their plight, and who could come to their assistance, alone and isolated as they were upon the vast and stormy ocean? But, *nil desperandum*. Imagine their joy when a sailor sent to the foretop to scan the stormy horizon was heard to cry, 'Strange sail on the weather bow!' The sound of mighty cheering rose above the tumult of the storm.

They hastily altered course, hoisted the distress flags and started firing the minute guns to attract the vessel's attention. At first there was no response, for the mighty sound of gunfire was lost in the violence of the storm. Then, to their utmost relief, the ship, which turned out to be the *Cambria*, a small British brig, acknowledged their signals and bore down. It was to be a case of David going to the aid of Goliath, for this vessel, commanded by Captain William Cook and carrying a team of Cornish miners and agents of the Anglo-Mexican Company, was a small brig of only 200 tons, whereas the *Kent* was a barque of seven times that burthen. Experienced officers aboard the bigger vessel, well aware of this situation, saw little prospect of all of them being saved.

For reasons of safety, the brig was obliged to remain a prudent distance from the distresssed ship, as some of the lower guns were being spontaneously activated in the heat and, furthermore, the *Kent* could explode at any moment and claim them all as victims. The excited passengers were urged to keep calm and obey orders. To re-inforce this message, military officers stood by with drawn swords, for panic at this stage as the ship's boats were being lowered would have been catastrophic. The captain commanded that the officers' ladies and soldiers' wives should board the first cutter, and the cool-headed, disciplined approach had a calming effect. Indeed, hardly a word was uttered,

The 'Kent' is left to her fate

apart from pitiful pleas from some wives to be left on board with their husbands, and even the babies kept quiet. Nevertheless, disaster almost overtook this well-controlled operation when one of the ship's cutters, crammed with passengers, was being lowered. Axemen had been positioned at the bow and stern to sever the ropes if one of them should fail to release at either end, thus preventing the occupants from being tipped into the sea. After a couple of abortive attempts to lower the fragile boat evenly on the undulating surface of the water, the command was eventually given to unhook. Then, horror of horrors, the tackle at the stern was cleared, but the ropes at the bow got entangled and the sailor was unable to cut through them with his axe. For several moments the fate of those who had survived thus far was poised between the devil and the deep blue sea. But Providence, in the guise of a sudden rogue wave, pushed up the stern, neatly enabling him to knock the tackle free.

If being allotted a place in one of the *Kent's* emergency lifeboats seemed like a welcome release for the shipwrecked, it also presented a new range of hazards. They found themselves being stowed beneath the seats and painfully thrust into all sorts of unlikely places to give the sailors enough room to ply the oars and as the seas broke over them, there was the paradoxical possibility of drowning *inside* a lifeboat. Mothers up to their necks in water tried to hold their babies safely above their heads throughout the painful 30 or 40 minutes it took to heave and toss their way through the stormy waters to their saviour ship. During the course of this operation, some of the men were forced into the choice of saving their children or their wives. A number of the shipwrecked were so petrified at the prospect of taking to the frail boats that they refused to leave the burning ship. Some made false leaps as they attempted to jump into the lifeboats, and were drowned. And then there was the greedy sailor who met his doom on account of being weighted down by hundreds of sovereigns he had plundered and secured in a handkerchief tied around his waist. By a cruel quirk of fate, the husband of the stowaway slipped as he tried to scramble aboard one of the cutters, and he was crushed to death between the heaving boat and the side of the brig as she looked on in horror. Three of the six cutters became swamped during the course of these manoeuvres.

When the survivors got alongside the *Cambria* the crew had great difficulty in getting them safely aboard, because many of them were so weak by now. However, a burly bunch of miners and Joseph Warren, the famous Cornish wrestler from St Just, who were travelling as passengers aboard the *Cambria*, distinguished themselves by taking up perilous positions, lifting the casualties bodily from the bouncing boats and passing them along a human chain up and over their heads to safety. Unfortunately, the compassionate wrestler injured his back in the process and was never able to wrestle again. A grateful lady passenger, who owed her life to him, paid him an annuity for the rest of his life. Throughout all this, most of the women, who it had been feared might cause problems with hysteria and panic, were credited with courage in the face of adversity. They obeyed orders and, when it came to being rescued, kept their nerve and chose the right moment to leap into the manly arms of their saviours aboard the brig. It was said that everyone willing to be rescued was taken off the *Kent* and that Captain Cobb was the last to leave his blazing ship.

At ten o'clock that night, when the *Cambria* had taken 547 souls safely aboard, the flames, which had spread along the upper deck and poop of the *Kent*, were leaping like greased lightning up the masts and along the rigging, illuminating the heavens and casting livid reflections upon the swirling seas. By a strange irony, the flags of distress continued to flutter valiantly amidst the leaping flames, until the masts burnt through and crashed into the ocean. But the horrifying and spectacular grand finale came just after midnight, when the eager flames finally reached the gunpowder. There was a tremendous explosion in a scene of fearful magnificence as sections of the burning barque were flung sky high, like a myriad of blazing rockets, or, as the poet said:

'Rose the shrill shriek, then all was hush'd,
Save the wild wind and the remorseless dash
Of billows.'

Next morning eleven soldiers who were caught in the blast were found clinging to the wreckage by Captain Bibby of the *Caroline*, who picked them up and landed them safely at Liverpool. But over 80 people lost their lives in the course of the drama.

Meanwhile, the gallant little brig, bearing 600 souls, which had so recently left Falmouth for a voyage to Mexico, headed back to the port with the wind in her tail. This was a merciful stroke of providence, for, shortly after anchoring, the wind veered to the north and, had it done so sooner, many of them would have perished through starvation and exposure. During this uncomfortable voyage Captain Cook, his passengers and crew generously and selflessly surrendered up their stores, cabins, spare clothing and every comfort for those they thought in greater need, reinforcing the finest humanitarian traditions of the sea. Furthermore, the milk of human kindness continued to flow in abundance when they landed at Falmouth; a fact placed on record by several letters of acknowledgement, including this one:

'Falmouth, March 16, 1825

GENTLEMEN,

In tracing the various links in that ample chain of mercy and bounty with which it has pleased a gracious Providence to surround the numerous individuals, lately rescued from the destruction of the Hon. Company's ship *Kent* – We, the Lieutenant Colonel commanding, and Officers belonging to the right wing of the 31st regiment, cannot but reflect with increasing gratitude on the beneficence of that arrangement whereby ourselves and our gallant men, after the awful and afflicting calamity that befel us, were cast upon the sympathies of the inhabitants of Falmouth and the adjacent towns; who have so widely opened their hands to provide for our numerous and pressing wants.

We were thrown on your shore as pennyless strangers, and ye took us in – we were hungry and ye gave us meat – naked and ye clothed us – sick and ye relieved and comforted us – we have found you rejoicing with those of us who have rejoiced, and weeping with such of us as have cause to weep – you have visited our fatherless and widows in their affliction, and sought by unceasing acts of the most seasonable, effective and delicate charity, to alleviate the measure of our suffering – Under such circumstances, what can we say, or where shall we find words to express our emotions? You have created between us and our beloved country, an additional bond of affection and gratitude, that will animate our future zeal: and enable us, amid all the vicissitudes of our professional life, to gratefully point our companions in arms to FALMOUTH, as one of the bright spots in our happy land, where the friendless shall find many friends, and the afflicted receive abundant consolation.'

(Signed by the officers)

The bravery of those concerned in the rescue was commemorated in a silver medal, struck by the inhabitants of Falmouth, Truro, Helston, Penryn and St Ives. It was also placed on record that a baby, 'Rob Roy' MacGregor, was born on the *Kent* during this disastrous voyage and safely landed at Falmouth.

15

An Epic Lifeboat Service

◆

'Late last night it became known that a large liner had gone ashore on rocks near Polpier Cove, the Lizard, in a thick fog, but no details could be procured as to the name and condition of the wreck. It has since transpired, however, that the vessel is the White Star liner Suevic, *from Sydney for Plymouth and London, and that she went ashore at 10.30 o'clock, after firing minute guns for some time. It is expected that there were 300 or 400 passengers aboard at the time.*

Shortly before midnight lifeboats were launched from the Lizard and Cadgwith, but none had returned at one o'clock, and as a red light was burning, probably for more assistance, the Mullion lifeboat was also summoned to be in readiness.

A special telegram to the West Briton *this morning states that the position of the* Suevic *on the Mainheer Rocks, near the Lizard lighthouse, is critical, and that the weather is bad. The vessel is afloat aft. There were about 800 passengers aboard when the vessel struck. Some of those had been landed, and at the time the message was despatched, tugs were taking off the remainder. All the Falmouth tugs were on the scene.'*

(The West Briton *18th March, 1907*).

For generations of seafarers returning to these much-loved shores after many months at sea, the sight of the Lizard Light was a reassuring one, welcoming them home. For Captain Thomas Jones, commander of the famous White Star Line's prestigious liner *Suevic*, homeward bound from Sydney on that fateful St Patrick's Day in 1907, the anticipated landfall was particularly poignant, for this was his last voyage. After 39 years of exemplary service, 17 of them in command of a ship, he was looking forward to a well-deserved retirement, but aware, no doubt, that a love and longing for ships and the sea would always be with him. The splendid 12,500 ton liner, with 524 passengers aboard, and carrying a valuable mixed cargo which included frozen meat, wool, leather, wheat and copper, had experienced a pleasant voyage until the

Sunday, when they ran into fog. The crew did not see the Ushant light as anticipated; then at about nine o'clock they saw an intermittent reflection of light in the distance, but eventually lost sight of it. About an hour and a half later the voice from the crow's nest hailed a reassuring 'All's well!', with the vessel under full steam at 14 knots. But, a few moments later, there was a frantic cry of 'Breakers ahead!' and almost immediately the liner struck the Stag Rocks and stranded on the three-quarter ebb tide. She was pierced almost directly under the mainmast, and her fore compartments soon filled with about 6 ft of water. Although she had settled in the bow, her stern section remained afloat.

If, as the Court of Inquiry later concluded, lack of proper seamanlike care had landed them on the rocks, the events which ensued were handled in calm, professional style by all concerned. Some of the passengers were asleep in their bunks, while others were enjoying traditional farewell celebrations, when the liner grated on the rocks and gave a disconcerting quiver from stem to stern. Whereupon the alarmed passengers made a scramble for the deck to see what had happened. They were reassured, told to keep quiet and obey instructions, while Captain Jones ordered the boats to be got ready for lowering. Distress rockets and fog lights were sent up, watertight compartments were closed down, and the bilge pumps activated.

Somewhat incongruously, Mrs Blair, a passenger who had been in the ship's hospital, was nearly thrown from her bunk when the impact came. But when she got to the door of the sick bay, a doctor said, 'Keep quiet; nothing has happened. We have only gone aground!' and a steward added, 'We have only struck a piece of wreckage!' Many of the passengers who had rushed on deck in their night attire, and others, hurried below to collect warm clothing, and returned resignedly to await their fate. Everyone, including the 85 children on the passenger list, behaved well and it was acknowledged that the women, many of whom had babies in their arms, displayed particular coolness and courage. While all this was going on, the captain mingled with the anxious passengers, urging them to keep calm, and personally supervising the lowering of the ship's lifeboats. Then it was a traditional case of women and children first, with stewards and officers handing out the lifebelts.

About half an hour after the stranding, the Lizard lifeboat signalled that she was on her way to the rescue. All the lifeboats in the area were summoned to assist that night but, as they launched into heavy seas, whipped up by a strong, south-westerly gale, would the brave lifeboatmen ever have guessed that they were about to enter the pages of history, in an all-time, epic lifeboat service? The Lizard lifeboat,

Locals salvage the 'Suevic's' washed up cargo

Admiral Sir George Back, under the command of second coxswain Edwin Mitchell, was the first to reach the scene, followed closely by the Cadgwith lifeboat, *Minnie Moon*, with coxswain Edward Rutter at the helm.

Back aboard the *Suevic*, heavy seas were hampering the attempts to get the loaded ship's boats safely away from the vessel's side and, after the first two had narrowly missed destruction, Captain Jones decided to await the arrival of the lifeboats from the shore, which was just as well, for they would never have survived the perils of the rocks and reefs in the hands of crewmen unfamiliar with this notorious coastline. Having discovered that two of the ship's boats had already been launched and successfully established contact with them, the Lizard lifeboat put a crewman aboard one of them, and towed her in to Polpeor, before returning to the stranded vessel. The second craft was picked up by the Cadgwith lifeboat. Then the Reverend Harry Vyvyan, the Honorary Secretary of that station, who was very much a man of action and a true man of the cloth, volunteered to pilot the craft ashore himself, so that his lifeboat would not be delayed in her urgent task of further rescue. He jumped aboard the ship's boat, which was towed clear of the *Suevic*, 100 yards to windward, then, casting off the tow, he took her safely through the dangerous, rock-strewn channel to the shore. Having landed twenty-five women and children, six sailors and an officer safely at Polpeor, he was keen to return to the scene of the emergency, using this boat. But the liner's plucky crew were inexperienced in these conditions and were not strong enough to row the rather unwieldy craft away from the shore against the pounding breakers, and the ship's boat was thrown onto a rocky ledge and partly stove in. Fortunately, Harry Vyvyan and the brave crewmen from the liner were able to get safely ashore. Nothing daunted, he continued his attempts to get her afloat, then called for more volunteers to launch the ship's other boat, which had been brought ashore by the Lizard lifeboat. But, as it happened he was able to get back to the wreck when the Lizard lifeboat returned after bringing in the third batch of survivors.

Mrs Duka, who came ashore in the first boat, carrying her baby son in her arms, said, 'The boat I was landed by was piloted by local men. Had the ship's crew not had their assistance our little craft must have been smashed to pieces, so rugged is the coast. Thirty women and children went ashore in that first boat. We had the water up to our knees, and landed in a drenched state. Brandy was given to us as soon as we reached the shore, and we then walked up to the hotel at the Lizard, where everything had been done for our comfort. The local men who received us on landing greeted us with cheers and joyful tears.

"Thank God," they said, "one boatload is saved!" We heard them cheering on the *Suevic*, too, for our safe arrival.'

The aforementioned Mrs Blair, who found herself amongst the fourth group to leave the distressed ship and put ashore by one of the Cornish lifeboats, said, 'We reached this boat by climbing down the rope ladder, and then sliding over a piece of hanging rope. The children – eight came ashore in my boat – were thrown into the men's arms. One woman, who was carrying a baby in her arms, slipped when getting over the ship's side, and fell into the boat. She cut her head and became unconscious. It was daybreak – about 7.30 – when we landed. Several Cornish folk were there to meet us. Two of our boatmen lost their oars, and we only got in with the assistance of a tug, which came after a lot of fuss. We were all drenched to the skin, and landed without a stick. I think the Cornish people are the most hospitable I ever met.'

The weather deteriorated as the night wore on but, nothing daunted, the Lizard and Cadgwith lifeboats, together with those of Coverack and Porthleven, continued a series of runs, aided and assisted by tugs from Falmouth. Conditions were at their worst at around three and four o'clock in the morning, when the high tide and incoming swells made it impossible to land at Polpeor. So subsequent boatloads of shipwrecked folk were diverted to Cadgwith, while the tugs returned to Falmouth with those they had saved. By these means all the passengers were safely landed by the following afternoon, and the officers and crew, apart from the captain and some senior officers, were landed by sunset. They stayed aboard with hopes of getting the vessel refloated, and to confer about salvage operations.

The locality was besieged, not only with the sudden influx of stranded passengers, but the hordes of curious sightseers, who appeared from all directions. By a strange irony, the only fatality throughout the whole affair concerned an over-excited sightseer. Twenty-two year old Benjamin Williams of Newlyn, who stopped off on the homeward waggonette to whet his whistle at the Blue Anchor, Helston, went for a joyride on a bicycle he found outside, then fell off and broke his neck.

The mass exodus began on Tuesday, and special trains were laid on by the Great Western Railway for those who had stayed overnight in villages around the Lizard and at Falmouth. Many of the crew, who had stayed at the Royal Cornwall Sailors' Home in Falmouth, left on the evening train, seen off by officials of the Seamen's Bethel and the Shipwrecked Mariners' Society, who had done so much to ease their plight. While the crew travelled northwards to Liverpool, the White Star Line were dispatching 160 salvage men southwards, to the scene of the stricken *Suevic*. Meanwhile, the Great Western Railway

Company's steamer *Antelope*, which had been sent down from Plymouth, had been making abortive attempts to get alongside the casualty, in unfavourable weather conditions. She eventually got alongside when the gale moderated, and removed the passengers' baggage. Local folk had a field day salvaging cargo strewn along the shore for the benefit of the Company, as well as indulging in a spot of beachcombing and souvenir hunting on their own account. In the event, the *Suevic's* after section, which was virtually intact, was cut away, towed to Southampton and aligned to a specially created bow section; whereupon she resumed her adventures.

The service records of the lifeboats involved indicate that 227 people were rescued by the Cadgwith lifeboat, 167 by the Lizard lifeboat, 44 by the Coverack lifeboat and 18 by the Porthleven lifeboat. The remaining 68 were landed by ships' boats and tugs. Saving so many people from one ship created a proud, all-time record for the area and for the RNLI, and it brought Silver Medals to the Cadgwith coxswain, Edward Rutter, and to the Revd Henry Vyvyan. Silver Medals also went to coxswain William Edward Mitchell and second coxswain Edwin Mitchell of the Lizard lifeboat, for their life-saving achievement, made in six trips from the shore, and to seamen George Anderson and William Williams of the *Suevic*, who distinguished themselves by carrying children and the sick down rope ladders and skilfully dropping them into the arms of waiting lifeboatmen on the bucking lifeboats. All who had sailed on that fateful voyage were able to enjoy a new lease of life, thanks to the skilled and heroic actions of those who risked theirs, in the heroic cause of saving life from shipwreck.

16

The Notorious *Lottery* Affair

◆

'There was small fry and big fish
A-waitin' to be caught;
With privateers an' smugglers
Indulgin' in the sport.'
(Old rhyme)

The heyday of smuggling was brought about in the 18th and early 19th centuries, after the increase in customs duties levied on such items as spirits, tobacco, perfumes, laces, silk and tea made the illicit importation of these goods a very profitable, though dangerous, prospect. When it came to enterprise, artfulness, skill and daring, none were more renowned than the seafarers of Cornwall, and when it came to swashbuckling exploits, the men of Cawsand and Polperro enjoyed a certain notoriety. Indeed, Polperro has the dubious distinction of being the place where the first station of the Coastguard Preventive Service was set up.

If nature had intended to create the perfect environment for the pursuit of freebooting, she could not have done better than the southern coast of Cornwall, with its rugged, indented coastline, wooded estuaries and inlets. Polperro, where a commodious creek led into a deep, secluded valley, of very difficult approach by land, was ideal for the purpose. The impoverished fisherfolk had wholeheartedly embraced this way of life, and many of their cottages had secret entrances, hiding places and concealed exits incorporated in them.

The event which achieved the greatest notoriety occurred during the traditional Yuletide season of peace on earth, and goodwill to all men. Perhaps the smugglers reckoned that the customs men would still be indulging in their Christmas festivities when they decided to bring the illicit goods ashore at Cawsand, on that fateful 26th December in 1798. But it seems that these officers had received a tip-off at around 10 pm, with regard to a certain smuggling vessel discharging her cargo off nearby Penlee Point. So the customs cutter *Hinde*, under the command of Mr Ambrose Bowden and four of his officers, promptly put to sea to investigate the matter.

On that clear and moonlit night, they soon discerned a very large smuggling cutter, with small boats alongside being loaded with goods, which were obviously about to be landed at Cawsand. But as soon as the miscreants spotted the advancing revenue cutter, they over-reacted, and a gruff, menacing voice rang out across the ruffled moonlit waters, audaciously warning the King's men that they had better keep off – or they would be fired upon! Bowden responded to this by boldly stepping forward, unfurling the revenue flag with a flourish, declaring that he was a revenue officer, and daring them to fire. Their hot-headed reaction on being thus cornered was to open fire on the revenue boat, and hope for an escape. After three shots had been fired, Bowden saw an oar fall from the hand of one of his officers, and heard the bowman exclaim, 'Glynn is shot!' Grabbing a musket, Bowden returned the fire, and a brisk volley ensued before the men aboard the smuggling vessel, which had been identified as the *Lottery*, cut her cable, and made sail to escape. With an injured officer on board, the *Hinde* was not in a postition to give chase. So she retrieved the anchor buoy which the smugglers had left behind in their haste, as potentially useful evidence, and proceeded to the naval frigate *Stag*, to seek medical assistance. But, sadly, the unfortunate officer, Humphrey Glynn, had died instantly, for the front part of his head had been completely shot away.

In those days, the more wily smugglers were adept at disguising their vessels in a variety of ways, including the implacement of false name plates, using different coloured sails and rather cheekily displaying registration numbers with the intention of being mistaken for revenue cutters. By one means or another, the *Lottery* and her villainous crew seem to have evaded all attempts at capture by the authorities, for several months. Then their luck ran out. For at about three o'clock on the thirteenth day of May the following year, as the *Hinde*, then under the command of Gabriel Bray, was cruising off the Start, a large cutter was observed, making for the shore. The revenue cutter came in very fast, and identified the vessel as the *Lottery*, although she had sacking obscuring her name. They were off the Bolt, when those aboard the errant ship realised what was happening and promptly put about and proceeded westwards. Sail was instantly made on board the revenue cutter, and there followed a most hectic and exhilarating chase down the entire length of the southern coast of Cornwall. Watchers on the shore must have been thrilled to witness such a graceful and spectacular display of speed and seamanship, which continued all through the night. But by dawn the next morning, when they were off the Lizard, and about five miles apart, they literally had the wind taken out of their sails, for their progress had been halted by a sudden calm. However, Captain Bray, not being willing to let the situation slip from his grasp at this late stage, dispatched two armed boats, under the command of his mate, Hugh Pearce, to take possession of the smugglers. Furthermore, he fired a gun from the *Hinde* and hoisted the revenue flag to the masthead, to show them that he meant business.

As these boats drew near, the crew of the *Lottery* were desperately plying their sweeps (operating long oars from a standing position), in an effort to get clear of trouble, and a gun was fired from her stern. She also hoisted English colours, and as soon as the revenue boats were within hailing distance, one of the smugglers raised a speaking trumpet to his lips and cried, 'Keep off, them boats, immediately!' Nothing daunted, Hugh Pearce rowed up to within less than a cable's length of the cutter, with the intention of making himself heard. He was warned again that if the boats did not keep off, they would be fired upon and sunk. Rising to his feet, Pearce shouted out, 'This is the *Hinde's* boat! My name is Pearce, and I have orders to board your vessel, which I must obey. I know that this cutter is the *Lottery*, and I also know the men on board.' Back came the bald reply, 'We don't care a damn who the boat belongs to, or who is in her. This vessel is not the *Lottery*, and unless you keep your boats off, we will fire into them and kill the lot of you!' Despite all this, Pearce made one final appeal to be permitted to come alongside, and said that if they co-operated with him, he would treat them well. The response was prompt and brutal. He was given to understand that if he attempted to board the vessel, not one of his party would live to return.

While this sharp exchange of views was taking place, some of the men on board the *Lottery* were running out a gun on the quarter nearest the boats, while two swivel guns were being aimed from the beam, and a man was standing by, armed with a musket. This being the situation, Pearce decided to return to the *Hinde*, for his men were alarmed and he thought it a better idea to tow the revenue cutter up to the smuggling vessel. At least, that is what he subsequently stated before a court of law. But, fortunately, Providence intervened, in the shape of a freshening breeze.

As that particular line of strategy had proved abortive, and the elements now indicated a return to their former tactics, the *Hinde*'s boats were hoisted aboard and sail was made on both vessels. The chase was on, once more, and the smugglers, seeing the revenue cutter drawing closer, jettisoned a quantity of spirits. However, despite the skilful manoeuvres of the smugglers, the *Hinde* continued to gain on them, and at about two o'clock in the afternoon, when they were off the Longships, the chase guns were brought to bear on the smuggling

The 'Hinde' in hot pursuit of the 'Lottery'

vessel, whose crew, realising that the game was up and not relishing being in the firing line themselves, lowered their sails. Twelve of them took to one of the ship's boats, and struck out rapidly towards the shore. But now that the tables were turned, Captain Bray despatched his two boats again. One took possession of the prize ship, which had five men aboard her at the time, while the other, with the mate aboard, gave chase to the ship's boat, which they captured when she was about halfway to the shore, together with the twelve men in her.

The prize ship, which was indeed the well-known smuggling vessel *Lottery*, was found to be laden with 716 casks and ankers of gin, as well as large quantities of tea and tobacco. As was customary in those days, when locally constructed vessels often changed hands between the hunters and the hunted, the *Lottery* was condemned, then, possibly adhering to the philosophy that it takes a thief to catch a thief, she was brought into Government service and employed as a revenue cutter in the English Channel. It was a strange circumstance that amongst the five men captured aboard the *Lottery* was a man named Pearce, but, as everyone swore that he had been merely a passenger, he was allowed to go free. The mate of the *Hinde* denied that this man was a relative of his, but pointed out that another customs officer aboard the revenue cutter, also called Pearce, was this man's son!

On capturing the *Lottery*, Captain Bray gave orders that the villainous crew should be placed in irons. The prize vessel was then taken into Plymouth, and it was expected that the smugglers would be speedily brought before the magistrates to face the consequences of their reckless actions. However, things took an unexpected turn when Roger Toms, one of the captured men, who had also been aboard the *Lottery* the previous December when the murder took place, made oath before a magistrate that Thomas Potter, who also stood indicted, had fired the shot which killed Humphrey Glynn, and that fellow prisoners William Searle and Thomas Ventin had aided and abetted him. Having turned informer, Roger Toms, who later admitted that he had given this account to save his life, was allowed to go free. The remaining fifteen smugglers were prosecuted before the magistrates, while five of them were destined to appear on more serious charges at the Old Bailey in London.

The judicial process in the sophisticated, faraway capital was effectively slowed down by some unexpected diversions, cunningly orchestrated by the loyal folk of Polperro, united in their freetrading interests and torn by a desire to help Thomas Potter and an overwhelming feeling of revulsion for the behaviour of Roger Toms. When it came to arresting Potter, the officers of the law found themselves to be continually frustrated, for the imperceptible bush-telegraph system, which warned of their approach, seemed always to be one jump ahead of them. So they sharpened their wits and reviewed their strategy, and thus it was that a stealthy band of soldiers, who approached from the west, surprised Potter in his own home, which, unfortunately for him, lacked the customary bolt hole at the rear, and took him prisoner. Arrangements went ahead for the trial of Thomas Potter, William Searle and Thomas Ventin at the Old Bailey in December 1799, to be charged with the wilful murder of Humphrey Glynn. But, in the event, it had to be postponed, owing to the absence of the principal witness, Roger Toms, for whom a search was instigated.

Soon after he had been released by the magistrates, on account of betraying Potter, Toms had been seen in the company of about 20 men, and then he disappeared. Whether he had gone to ground voluntarily, knowing how he stood with his own folk, was uncertain, but rumour had it that some smugglers had imprisoned him in a cave somewhere on the Cornish coast to prevent him from appearing as a witness against the prisoners at the bar. Now that the authorities had flushed out Potter and removed him to London for greater security, the folk of Polperro gave their wholehearted attentions to Toms, who by this time had been found and taken aboard a revenue cutter at Fowey to protect him from the vengeance of his late associates, and to make sure of his appearance in court on behalf of the Crown. As far as the smuggling fraternity was concerned, it was a desperate situation, calling for all the artfulness and cunning they could muster. They made approaches to Roger Toms's good lady and, with the aid of pleas, threats and solemn promises that her husband should come to no harm, Mrs Toms was persuaded to take part in a trick which involved a rendezvous with her husband at Polruan. Toms was similarly inveigled ashore, and the outcome was that a party of men leapt out at him from behind a hedge and carried him off as the couple were walking across Lantic Down in the gathering twilight. Nevertheless, in the tradition of there being honour among rogues, it was said that they treated him with every consideration, in faithful fulfilment of their promise, as they moved him from place to place, prior to taking him across to Guernsey, before dispatching him to America. The transatlantic vessel was on the point of sailing, when, at the very last moment, Toms succeeded in making himself known to the Government authorities, who were searching for him

On 10th December 1800, just two years after the firing of the fatal shot off Cawsand. Thomas Potter, William Searle and Thomas Ventin stood in the Justice Hall of the Old Bailey, charged with the wilful murder of Humphrey Glynn, on 26th December 1798. The most important evidence was that of Roger Toms, who deposed that he was a mariner on board the *Lottery* on the night in question. He said that the cargo consisted of spirits, and that they had winched several boatloads to Cawsand before he went below. While between decks, he heard some voices cry out, 'Keep off!' and afterwards heard repeated, 'It's a King's boat!' Firing then took place and, presently, orders were given to cut the cable, and they ran before the wind towards Polperro, where they arrived at about twelve o'clock. A conversation then took place between Oliver, the master, Potter, Searle and someone else, with Oliver saying that they would be sorry if any harm had resulted from their firing. Potter replied that he had taken good level when he fired, and was sure that he saw a man drop. Toms then went on to say that at the time of the firing, Ventin, who was the cook, was sent below by Oliver, to make the pokers red hot in preparation for firing the swivels, if necessary. Toms testified that he went on deck after the cable had been cut, and heard Searle say that he was glad that the boat had been kept off and that, although he had fired, he had meant to do no harm, and hoped that he had not done any harm. Toms confirmed that the buoy produced in court was, indeed, from the *Lottery*.

In response to this, the counsel for the defence, Mr Gurney, said that Toms was not a person whose evidence on oath could be believed, and he called on three Cornishmen to affirm that they knew him, and that he had the reputation of being a thief and a liar, and that his evidence, even under oath, was not to be relied upon. However, these witnesses found themselves being subjected to a severe cross-examination, calculated to show that they, in common with everyone else on the coast, were smugglers themselves, and therefore only interested in protecting the prisoners. The jury, after retiring for less than an hour, returned a verdict of guilty against Potter, and acquitted Searle and Ventin on the charge of murder. They were, instead, found guilty of 'firing a certain gun, or swivel, and directing certain other firearms, and obstructing certain officers in the service of the Customs . . .' They were sentenced to be confined to 'hard labour upon the River Thames for two years.'

Sir William Scott then pronounced sentence in the usual way and, having addressed the prisoner at some length, concluded, 'You will be conveyed to the place of execution, there to be hanged until you are dead, your body to be given to be anatomized (dissected for analysis).' Because of the state of the tide, the unfortunate man was respited for a week. Then on 18th December he met his grim fate at Execution Dock. He was attended by a Roman Catholic priest, and it was said that he conducted himself with great penitence and that he met his end with becoming resignation and sincere contrition.

Potter's widow, who had a reputation for being hard-hearted, survived her spouse by many years. A century ago, one old crone of Polperro recalled, 'When 'er went up ter Lunnen town ter see 'er 'usband, afore 'e were 'ung, and se'ed a silk 'an'kerchif 'angin' round 'is neck, 'er asked 'im ter give un to 'er, as 'er thought as 'ow it were too good a thing ter be lost.' Old Pol Potter died in 1841, and lies in the churchyard at Lansallos, while the murdered Humphrey Glynn, for whom her husband had paid the price with his life, was buried at Maker, in the parish of Kingsand.

One of the smugglers involved in this notorious event went on to secure a place in history a few months later. For he was shot dead during a smuggling affray off these shores, apparently by a customs officer, and his final exploit was recorded on his headstone in Talland church thus:

'Erected
To the memory of
Robert Mark
late of Polperro, who, was unfortunately
shot at sea, the 24th of January
in the year of our Lord God
1802, in the 40th year of his age.

. . . .

In prime of life most suddenly
Sad tidings to relate
Here view my utter destiny
And pity my sad fate.
I, by a shot that rapid flew
Was instantly struck dead
Lord pardon the offender who
My precious blood did shed
Grant him to rest and forgive me
All I have done amiss
And that I may rewarded be
With everlasting bliss'

17

The Fate and Legacy of HMS *Anson*

♦

HMS *Anson*, which was built as a third rate 64-gun frigate in Plymouth in 1780, and launched on 4th September the following year, was a well seasoned vessel, which had taken part in many a daring skirmish on behalf of king and country. She had fought in the Battle of the Saints in 1782, taken part in the Expedition to Quebec and assisted in the capture of the 40-gun French ship *Etoile* in 1795. In the next five years she added to her laurels by capturing the 40-gun French *Loire*, and the Spanish *Salvador*. The year 1807 started promisingly enough, for New Year's Day saw her in triumph at the capture of Curaçao. But these glorious events were eclipsed by her final, fateful encounter with the notorious maritime trap of Mount's Bay, which earned her a place in British naval history, and gave rise to a beneficial, humanitarian legacy for seafarers the world over.

Captain Lydiard, who had joined the Navy in 1780, became a lieutenant 14 years later, and served aboard *The Captain* and the *Southampton*, where he demonstrated an impetuosity and daring in battle. This led to his immediate command of a prize ship which he had captured, and the eventual promotion to captain. Then in 1805, when he was 36 years of age, he was given command of HMS *Anson*, which had been cut down to a 44-gun frigate with a poop, and reduced to fifth class. Not long after returning from the heady triumphs of Curaçao, this much-used old lady of war was commissioned as a look-out vessel for the Channel Fleet, to be stationed off Brest. As Captain Lydiard's friend and first lieutenant had just been promoted to the rank of Commander, and was awaiting a posting, he was invited to enjoy a cruise aboard HMS *Anson* as his personal guest.

On the morning of 23rd December 1807, HMS *Anson* sailed into Falmouth harbour to join the rest of the fleet and, soon after coming to anchor, Captain Lydiard and First Lieutenant Thomas Ball Sullivan, who lived at Mylor, went ashore to meet up with the other captains and high-ranking officers. Fulfilling a stylish social role was an integral part of their duties; useful for making the right kind of contacts, in regard to promotion and the prudent marriage stakes. 'Where shall we dine tonight?' said one. 'You would be very welcome to dine aboard my ship,' said Captain Lydiard. 'Captain James has invited us to Woodlands. All the captains in the harbour are expected to dine there tonight,' they were told. So that is what happened, and a good time was enjoyed by one and all, but did it influence subsequent events?

At the court martial questions were asked as to why the small bower cable, which parted and contributed to the disaster, had not been spliced before HMS *Anson* left Falmouth, and why the new sheet cable, acquired while they were in port, had not been bent. But it was said that the captain was so keen to put to sea that night, that he did not wish to delay the unmooring. It just so happened that one Henry Cuttance, an innkeeper and smuggler of Gunwalloe, who was in Falmouth that Christmas Eve, noticed the *Anson* being towed out of harbour by her own boats. He had good reason for a heightened awareness of Royal Navy manoeuvres, having recently been press-ganged, and having achieved a very daring escape from a vessel several miles out at sea, by the expedient of leaping overboard and swimming to the shore. 'There, but for the grace of God, go I!' he told his cronies in the bar parlour of the Halzephron Inn afterwards, also congratulating himself on his deliverance. But little did any of them imagine the fearful significance of these and subsequent events, which would be recounted by local cottage firesides on stormy winter evenings for generations to come.

On Christmas Day the south-westerly winds veered and intensified to hurricane force over the next few days, creating mountainous seas in Mount's Bay, and diabolical conditions for sailing vessels, which could so easily find themselves being driven helplessly on shore before the wind. This was a situation only too well known to the local seafaring fraternity, who instinctively kept watch for vessels in distress. When a large ship was reported to be in difficulties off Gunwalloe on the afternoon of 28th December, Henry Cuttance immediately recognised her as the *Anson*. So what had been happening to her in the meantime? HMS *Anson* had encountered increasingly difficult conditions after leaving the shelter of Falmouth haven to take up her position as a look-out ship at this time of renewed agitation with the French. On the night of the 27th, they were about four leagues south-south-east of the island of Bas, where they lay off, under close-reefed main topsail and reefed canvas. But by next morning the west-north-westerly winds had veered to the south-west and increased to hurricane force, and the weather had thickened and drastically reduced their visibility. Tremendous seas were running and the seasoned old vessel was taking in water at the rate of about eight inches an hour. There was some difference of opinion as to their exact position in these diabolical conditions, but Captain Lydiard considered that the most responsible course of action was to return to the shelter of Falmouth haven. The story might have ended here, had not gaps appeared in the all-enveloping mist and the jutting coastline of Land's End been mistaken for the Stagg Rocks, off the Lizard.

Violent storms, sudden blanketing by fog, the mistaking of one headland for another, all have led to the wrecking of countless ships on the southern coast of Cornwall over the centuries. *The Times* reported:

'The *Anson* sailed for Falmouth on Christmas Eve, for her station off the Black Rocks, as one of the look-out frigates of the Channel Fleet. In the violent storm of Monday, blowing about W. to S.W., she stood across the entrance of the Channel, towards Scilly, made the Land's End, which they mistook for the Lizard, and bore up, as they thought for Falmouth. Still doubtful, however, in the morning of Monday, Captain Lydiard stood off again to the southward; whence a consultation being held, it was once more resolved to bear up for Falmouth. Running eastward and northward, still under the fatal persuasion that the Lizard was on the north west of them, they did not discover the mistake till the man on the look-out ahead, called out "breakers!"'

It was a terrifying situation, and they soon realised that they had become embayed. Lieutenant Thomas Gill told the court martial, 'We immediately wore and hauled to the wind on the larboard tack. It was then resolved to come to anchor about five. After having furled everything, we let go the best bower [one of two anchors carried at the ship's bow]. She took the cable entirely to the clinch; she rode by this cable till four o'clock on the morning of the 29th, and then parted. We immediately let go the small bower which brought up at the clinch also: by this cable we rode until half past seven, when she parted, and it was resolved to run her on shore.' So, as it transpired, the cable, with all the masts standing, had held for twelve hours, during which time the vessel was pitching heavily and two hand pumps and a chain pump were constantly at work. Hugh Steward, master of the vessel said, 'It was blowing very hard, the ship pitching forecastle under, and so tremendous a sea as I never saw in my life.' There was apparently no consultation about whether anchoring would have provided the best possible chance of saving the ship and her crew, or whether the masts should have been cut away in an effort to ride out the storm. The captain determined to run the ship on shore rather than endeavouring to bring her up by the sheet anchor and cutting away the mast, because

Captain Lydiard distressed by the scene

he feared that the vessel might have veered into an irretrievable situation. The land was not visible when the decision was made to run the ship ashore, but they had seen the rocky coastline and a seemingly more benign ridge of sand the previous night, and decided to make for that. The captain had not left the deck from the time of the first cable parting.

As the crew of the stricken ship strove desperately to achieve a controlled beaching in these wild conditions, those who had assembled along the shore could only stand in helpless horror, as the once proud vessel, which had emerged triumphant on so many occasions, was overcome in her final battle – with the elements. In a conflict of wind and wave and tide and current, she struck the ground. Then she went broadside-on to the shore and heeled over, with gigantic seas breaking over her. This dramatic turn of events gave way to a scene of the utmost pathos and confusion, where the cries of anguished humanity and the crushing of ship's timbers mingled with the howling of the hurricane and the relentless, deafening, thundering of the surf upon the notorious Loe Bar, which had claimed so many ships before. 'Never did the sea run more tremendously high,' it was said of this area renowned for its storms. It broke over the vessel with such force that the masts soon went by the board, and it soon became a classic case of every man for himself. The officers and men who had made a dash for the poop, regarding it as the highest and safest place to be, were soon swept away. Many more were carried off by the swirling waters which swamped the deck and rigging, while others became the victims of falling spars and flying debris. By a merciful quirk of fate in a diabolical situation, the mainmast fell in such a way as to form a bridge from the ship to the shore above the reflux of the surf. Most of those who survived escaped by this means, having successfully anticipated the movement of the waves and chosen the right moment to run along the slippery mast. But many who attempted to escape from the rigging, or who cast their fate to the winds by jumping into the surf, were swept to eternity by the powerful undertow as they attempted to scramble up the beach. Hugh Steward, who had observed all this, watched the recession of the waves, then leapt upon the beach. He threw himself on his face and dug and clawed his hands into the sand with all his force as the waves crashed over him. Then as they scoured back, he leapt up and ran and skilfully repeated this performance until he was pulled to the safety of the shore.

Another survivor, who claimed to have been near Captain Lydiard on the main mast, said that he seemed to have lost the use of his faculties in the horror of the scene. Another report tells of Captain Lydiard and his former first lieutenant being lashed to the stanchion of the wheel, while the surgeon, Robert Smith, and his son, who was a very young midshipman, were lashed to the gun tackles near the wheel, on the weather side of the ship. Then a terrific sea suddenly flung the lad across the deck with such violence as to kill him. As his father instinctively freed himself to go to his aid, he was similarly battered to death by the waves. About three quarters of an hour after the vessel had struck, when he assumed that all had left the ship, Captain Lydiard said, 'Sullivan, it is our turn now. You go first.' As they were watching the movement of the waves and about to make a run for the main mast, they spotted one of the ship's boys clinging to the gear round the stump. Commander Sullivan had the presence of mind to drop cross-legged onto the mast and cling to the ropes as the next wave came, but when he looked around he saw that the captain and the boy had been swept away. Those on the beach thought that he was trying to encourage the boy to escape at the time, and at the court martial it was said that he was too exhausted to get through the surf. As soon as the captain lost his life, the command of the ship devolved on Hugh Steward, and a heavy mantle of responsibility descended on the shoulders of Lieutenant Thomas Gill.

Having escaped the trauma of a shipwreck, it must take a very special kind of courage to risk one's life again by returning to the scene as humane seaman, Richard Henley, did. The spectators on the shore were filled with admiration for the bravery of this young member of the gunnery crew, and the intrepid local heroes who ventured out through the thundering surf. Between them they succeeded in rescuing victims from the rigging, injured sailors, as well as women and children trapped down below and a number of errant crewmen who had been clapped in irons for some misdemeanour and left to their fate.

Mr Tobias Roberts, an ironmonger and saddler from Helston, who was a powerful swimmer, seized a rope and struck out boldly through the hazardous surf, towards the stricken vessel, which was fast disintegrating. After being buffeted about for some time and almost suffocated by the spray, he managed to attach a rope to the wreck and establish a lifeline. He and Methodist lay preacher, Mr Foxwell of Mullion, who also ventured his life through the surf, had children handed to them from the sinking ship. They both attempted to wade ashore with a child under one arm, hanging on to the rope by the other. After a few moments they were engulfed by a terrific wave, which knocked Tobias Roberts off his feet. Mr Foxwell, who had maintained his grip on the rope, was able to grasp him by the collar, enabling him to regain his balance and reach the safety of the shore with the child.

The *Anson*, which had struck at about 8 am on that fateful morning, went to pieces at about 2 pm, and disappeared about an hour later. Bodies were strewn all over the place, and continued to be washed in over the next few days. The beach was covered with wreckage, casks of rum and other valuable cargo, and revenue officers and the militia from Helston were promptly summoned to take charge of the situation. Salvaged personal belongings, such as watches and jewellery, were laid out at the Fishmonger's Arms in Porthleven, under armed guard.

Some of the survivors, bleeding, battered and bewildered, many of them half-naked, were taken over the cliff to Porthleven, where local folk provided them with sustenance and dry clothing. But most were taken to Helston, where they were cared for by the magistrates, and later sent to Falmouth, in charge of the Regulatory Captain at that port. However, some of the crew, who regarded this as a heaven-sent opportunity to release themselves from the confines of the Royal Navy, took to their heels and scampered off over the hills the moment they reached the shore. Among those who survived were Commander Sullivan, Lieutenant Thomas Gill, Mr Hugh Steward, master, Mr Ross, the assistant surgeon and midshipmen Hill and Braily. As soon as Captain James of Woodlands heard of the disaster, he visited the scene and took the surviving officers back to his home. Most of the victims of this shipwreck were buried in a huge pit above the beach at the eastern end of Loe Bar, where a gigantic cross was later emplaced. Robert Smith, the surgeon, and Richard Leech, an eleven year old midshipman aboard the frigate lie buried in the churchyard of St Michael's, Helston, where the headstone tells us that from a complement of 301 persons, including four women and three children, 171 survived, twelve supposedly deserted, and the remainder perished. The body of Captain Lydiard, which was washed ashore and picked up by Mr Edward Pascoe of Porthleven, was taken to Falmouth and interred with full military honours. But it was exhumed a month later, and reburied in the family vault at Haslemere.

When the captain lost his life, at about 8.45 am on the morning of 29th December 1807, the responsibility for all that had transpired fell on Lieutenant Thomas Gill and the master, Hugh Steward, who were tried by court martial aboard HMS *Salvador de Mundo* in Hamoaze (Plymouth) on Tuesday 5th January 1808. They came to the verdict that HMS *Anson*, which was endeavouring to make the shore in a violent gale and thick weather rather than riding out the storm, was not in a state of readiness to come to anchor when upon a lee shore in such conditions as the ship had to encounter. They concluded that no blame should be attached to any of the surviving officers, apart from Mr Hugh Steward, who was duly admonished.

The harrowing experience of standing helplessly on the shore, seeing so many lives being lost, seemingly so needlessly, when apparently so close to help, had such a profound effect on Henry Trengrouse of

Helston, that he devoted the rest of his days to the designing of an effective life-saving apparatus for use in inshore rescues. It was said that a local fireworks display in honour of King George III's birthday set him thinking about the possibility of a rocket firing a line to a stranded vessel, as a means of establishing contact. A similar idea had occurred to Lieutenant John Bell in 1791, and in 1807 Captain G.W. Manby had been experimenting with a mortar for firing a shot. But, although Manby was awarded £2,000 by the Government for his invention, it was cumbersome and dangerous and had to be withdrawn after fatalities occurred during testing. Trengrouse's ingenious invention fitted neatly into a box measuring 4 ft 3 inches by 1 ft 6 inches, which meant that it could be conveniently carried on a ship, or transported over cliffs to the scene of an emergency. His apparatus was lighter and more efficient, for the velocity of a rocket increased gradually and was therefore less likely to snap the line than the sudden, violent action of the mortar, and the illumination of its trail had a distinct advantage at night, when most emergencies occurred. Furthermore, Trengrouse's apparatus could be fired from shore to ship, or from ship to shore, which, by the nature of things usually meant following the direction of wind and weather, and offered a wider margin of success.

Having devised an apparatus with the potential for saving hundreds of lives each year, he set about trying to promote it, by writing features for the press and contacting Government officials. But, in the event, it was a frustrating ten years before he was able to carry out a demonstration for Admiral Sir Charles Rowley, and other high-ranking naval officers. He was subsequently awarded a Silver Medal and 30 guineas by the Society of Arts, after carrying out experiments in Hyde Park in London, proving that a rocket 1¾ inches in diameter could carry a cord across the Serpentine. The Government eventually ordered 20 sets of equipment, insisting they should be manufactured by the Ordnance Department and allowing him a fee of just 50 guineas. Recognition for his skills also came from the Czar of Russia, in the form of a diamond ring. However, he had paid a heavy price for his unfaltering idealistic vision in terms of declining livelihood, financial outlay and his health.

Even if he did not reap material rewards for his labour of love, or immediate recognition, he was well aware of the worth of his endeavours, and on his deathbed he told his son, 'If you live to be as old as I am, you will find my rocket apparatus all along our shores.' And he was right. To Henry Trengrouse, above all others, humanity has been indebted for an invention which has preserved countless lives from shipwreck, the world over. And all this came about on account of witnessing the harrowing shipwreck of HMS *Anson* on that cruel December morning on Loe Bar.

18

The Sailor's Ghost

◆

When Jimmy Botterel of St Just was a young lad, he would stand on the Penwith shores, gazing longingly out across the wild Atlantic Ocean and dreaming of the day he would grow up and sail the Seven Seas. When Jimmy was a sailor, serving aboard privateers at the time of Napoleon, he would yearn for landfall, his cosy cottage fireside, and the girls he had left behind. When Jimmy was an old man, he moved to a new home, further up that coast, where he could see the sea and recall the happy adventures and warm comradeship of a life on the ocean wave.

If Old Jimmy expected that all was set fair in his retirement, this doughty old sea-dog was in for a disappointment, at least initially. For, shortly after leaving the sea, he became troubled by a strange phenomenon, in the form of a close friend and old shipmate called John Jones, who had been drowned at sea. It had been the sort of wild and stormy night that this Atlantic coast knows all too well, and in the very early dawning, he was aroused by three loud taps on his bedroom window. When he opened his eyes he beheld the ghost of his former shipmate, looking pale and sad, and seeming to be dripping wet, amid a quivering, misty aura. Then it suddenly disappeared. Jimmy was petrified, but eventually lapsed back into fitful sleep. In the sober light of morning, he tried to convince himself that this vivid experience had only been a dream. But things got worse. Over the next week or so the spectre became more persistent, following him around wherever he went, even in broad daylight, with an expression on its wavery face that seemed to become more menacing and accusing. How could someone, to whom he had once been so close, haunt him in this way and look so angry and reproachful? It scared the living daylights out of Jimmy, who could find no means of escape.

Jimmy's friends noticed that the cheerful old salt had suddenly become pale and withdrawn. Could he possibly be in love? No, it looked more drastic than that. 'Jimmy,' they said, 'You've gone some quiet all of a sudden, boy. You're wanderin' around all by yourself, lookin' like wot you seen a ghost!' 'I 'ave seen a ghost. The ghost of my ole shipmate Jack Jones, wot's always bin like a brother to me; 'e 'ave come to 'aunt me.' They were amazed, but tried to reassure him by saying that ghostly friends could mean no harm. 'Why don't 'e speak to 'un?' they asked. 'I be fair quakin'. Me knees is a shakin' and if I tried to open me mouth, 'tis sure the words would never come out.' Old Morval, who lived at a neighbouring farm and had dealings with pellars (wise men), looked thoughtful, then declared that he'd heard tell that spectres never spoke until they were spoken to. 'Maybe there's somethin' 'e want done, as 'e can't do 'isself. Like if 'e got drownded in a 'urry,' said Old Zebediah. And everyone agreed with this. Old Morval went so far as to warn him that spirits got angry when frustrated by being unable to communicate their wishes.

So the next time that ghostly Jack appeared, looking sad, then increasingly angry, Jimmy plucked up his courage and blurted out, 'Jack Jones, me dear ole shipmate. Tell me wot I can do to give 'e rest an' peace.' In quavering tones, most unlike his firm, manly, mortal voice, the ghost of Old Jack replied, ''Tis well that thou hast spoken, for 'twould've been the death of 'e for sure, had'st thou held thy tongue ere long. Wot 'urt an' vexed me most, me dear ole comrade, was that thou seemest to fear the one wot was like a brother to 'e: the best of all shipmates.' Jimmy, feeling reassured by this, declared, 'I only wish I could grasp 'e firmly by the hand, an take 'e for a pint or two in the tavern, jus' like we done in the good ole days. Us 'ad some fair ole rollickin' times, didn't us?' Phantom Jack smiled and said, 'That's more like it, me ole mate. That's more like your cheerful ole self again. Dear Jimmy; a staunch and true friend in life an' in death. Listen carefully now, an' I will tell 'e why I come. It's like this 'ere. That stormy winter's night when I first appeared to 'e at your bedside some weeks since, I 'ad bin aboard a' Indiaman in the Bay o' Biscay, an' a fair ole storm it were too. Us've bin through some rare ole storms and skirmishes together, but this one boded ill. "Clew up the mains'l," sings out the cap'n. So there am I, drawin' the lower ends of the sails to the upper yard, ready for furlin', with the ole vessel 'eavin' an' rollin' away in these 'ere 'igh winds and moun'ainous seas, when all of a sudden she gives this mighty lurch. So wot 'appens? I loses me grip, falls overboard and gets drownded afore anyone knows I've gone. 'Tis true wot they says; 'twas really quite a pleasant feelin', drowndin'. Down, down, down I goes through the water. Seems like an eternity. All me life, it flashed afore me. An' I thought o' all me ole shipmates. An' most of all I thought of 'e, dear Jimmy, me finest mate, an' all the 'appy times wot we 'ad spent together. But as all me ole shipmates as 'ad slipped their anchors afore me rushed to welcome me to Fiddler's Green, it troubled

The ghost of John Jones

me ter think o' all the unfinished business as I 'ad left be'ind me, 'ere on earth.'

Old Jimmy gaped open mouth at his suddenly talkative, ghostly comrade, and wanted to know more about Fiddler's Green, the sailors' heaven. But the phantom brushed aside his volley of questions, merely assuring him all would be well, and that a true hearted sailor had nothing to fear. 'Let me tell 'e about this 'ere unfinished business. It's like this. Most of my prize money and possessions lie in an ole seamen's chest left at that ole public 'ouse wot us used to frequent down by the docks in fair Plymouth town. I want 'e to go there an' collect my chest. I want 'e to take it to another 'ouse, pay off my debts to the folk wot 'ad looked ar'ter me so well, all around Plymouth, then the rest be yourn.' 'But how . . ?' began Jimmy, looking agitated. 'Keep calm, me ole mate. 'Tis time to go. Ride over to Plymouth in 'aste, and I'll meet 'e there and tell 'e wot to do next.' 'Of course I'll do that for 'e,' said Jimmy, unthinkingly reaching out for that once familiar hand, which was not there, and gazing into those melancholy eyes, which used to be so full of life and merriment. They lit up briefly as Jack's ghost declared, 'Until us meets again, I wish 'e well,' then vanished.

Old Jimmy was up with the lark next morning, and rode on a borrowed nag in the direction of Plymouth, scene of many of his youthful, naval exploits. It was time to light up the candles on the second night when he eventually reached the fair city just across the Tamar. He found lodgings close to the inn where his comrade Jack had left all his worldly possessions, and clambered thankfully into the well-worn feather bed. Weary as he was, he lay awake musing about the tasks ahead. Then he gradually became aware of the ghostly form of Jack at his bedside. 'Oh, Jack, I be a tossin' and turnin' on account o' frettin' about the things I 'ave ter do fer 'e.' 'Pray, do not fret, dear comrade. All will be well. The landlady knew us both, as brothers, sharin' clothes and money, and 'elpin' each other in times o' need. She will not know as wot I'm drownded, nor that a fair fortune lurks in that battered ole chest. So if 'e tells 'er as wot I'm in town, and will call to see 'er afore I sails, she'll let 'e carry off the chest. Bring it 'ere, and I'll show 'e wot's ter be done next. And now, good night, me dear ole mate.' And then he vanished again.

The cheerful, buxom landlady was pleased to see Old Jimmy, and was glad to part company with the scruffy old chest that had been littering up her hall for too long. 'Give me love to dear Cap'n Jones,' she said, as Old Jimmy staggered off with the heavy chest. 'Can't think what 'e keeps in there. The key to me 'eart p'raps. 'E's welcome to that any time. Fine figure of a man is our Cap'n Jones. 'E could make an 'onest woman out o' me, any day. Jus' tell 'im as Ada sends 'er love, and to be sure to call and see me afore 'e leaves port.'

Old Jimmy humped his precious load through back streets and alleyways, keeping a sharp eye out for cut-throats and villains. He heaved a sigh of relief when he reached his lodgings, and stretched and straightened his back before he knelt and opened it. At first all he could see was smart and spanking new seafaring kit, which was puzzling, for it did not weigh very much. Then he realised that the trunk had a false bottom, and that stacks of gleaming coins and precious trophies were concealed in secret drawers in the skibbet. Then ghostly Jack appeared, and explained just what had to be done. He accompanied Jimmy on all his visits around the port, visible to him but invisible to others, until all the outstanding business that had troubled him in paradise had been neatly settled. Then he evaporated into thin air, without saying 'goodbye'.

Jimmy, who had become accustomed to his dear old mate's eerie company, wondered whether he had seen the last of him. But no, when he was down by the docks, admiring the shipping and feeling the poignant pull of the sea – and regret for his lost youth – he heard a faint rustle, then turned and saw Jack close beside him. But this was a very different Jack, for had he been visible to the other people milling around, they would have mistaken him for a young able seaman, resplendent in a brand new naval uniform, looking full of life and zest. 'I've just bin to our ole inn,' he said, in a strong and youthful voice. 'Kissed me 'and to our ole landlady through the open winder, and done a bunk afore 'er could reach the door to welcome 'ome 'er favourite sailor boy. 'Er 'ave bin 'opin' ter lead me to the altar these many year, so bein' a ghost do 'ave its advantages, dear Jimmy.' But his old mate was not so sure about that, yet.

They walked and glided on in silence, until they reached a handsome barquentine, surrounded by all the hustle and bustle that went with the departure of an ocean-going vessel before a long voyage. This made old Jimmy long even more to be a young man again, and as he turned around to look at his companion, ghostly Jack looked deep and sorrowfully into his eyes. 'I bid 'e farewell, dear Jimmy, for I'm off to sea once more. There truly be advantages for bein' immortal, for now I can share my time a'tween Fiddler's Green an' the chosen ships o' mortal men. For we be the guardian spirits o' chosen vessels, and vessels 'aunted by the ghosts o' seafarers drownded are seldom wrecked, for we forewarn o' tempests and other perils o' the deep.' 'Shall I never see 'e again, dear Jack?' asked Jimmy, rather sadly. 'Not in life, but if 'e think of yer ole mate as yer breath leaves yer body and 'e pass from this world to the next, I'll be there ter welcome 'e ter Fiddler's Green. Though my clay do lie deep in the Bay o' Biscay, your'n will repose, me ole mate, in the churchyard at Zennor. But we'll meet in the sailors' heaven, an' roam the Seven Seas for ever more! For as I told 'e, a staunch an' true 'earted Jolly Jack Tar do 'ave nothin' ter fear. 'Till then, adieu.' So saying, he glided aboard the barquentine and vanished.

Old Jimmy was left to make his reflective way home with the poor old nag, who was so weighed down with these unexpected earthly riches that he died of exhaustion shortly afterwards. It took much longer to make this homeward journey, over hills and moors and through the narrow lanes of Cornwall, but his spirits rose when he beheld the hills of home, and the sparkling waters of the dreamy, blue Atlantic far beyond. And did he not have a smart new set of clothes in his pannier bags; coins and treasures enough to last him for the rest of his days? Then, when his mortal days were ended, would he not join dear old Jack and his other seafaring comrades, where vibrant, ultramarine oceans were forever calm, the fruit forever ripe for the tasting, and the flowers perpetually in bloom? There would be singing and dancing and all the other things that seafarers enjoyed, to delight them throughout eternity. But if things ever seemed a little too dull and a little too perfect, he could always haunt a ship or two, and enjoy a life on the jolly old ocean wave, as he had done so happily since he was a lad.

19

Strange Happenings at Godrevy

◆

Before they built the lighthouse on Godrevy Island, the dangerous reef of rocks, lying off the most easterly point of St Ives Bay and known somewhat innocuously as 'The Stones', was a deadly trap for navigation. One of the earliest disasters on record occurred here on the day that Charles I was executed in London, when the French-bound *Garland* of Topsham, which had been riding at anchor in St Ives Bay, was driven helplessly onto these rocks in a tempest. This was rather strange, for the vessel was carrying the clothes and personal effects of the Prince of Wales (later King Charles II) and the Queen. It became immortalised as 'Prince Charles' Wardrobe Wreck'. This spectacular occurrence gave rise to some enthusiastic beachcombing. Many of the valuables were seized by the Arundells, who were lords of the manor, and the militia, but tradition says that the Queen's priceless jewels were discovered on the Gwithian shore by a humble villager.

Gleaning the bounty of the sea had long been traditional around these parts, for this impoverished, but sturdy, breed, well-used to disasters at sea, reckoned that the ocean, which claimed its victims, would also yield up its treasures. Furthermore, they felt privileged if Neptune chose to deposit the bounty of the sea on their particular strand; hence the apocryphal prayer, 'Lord, we do not pray for wrecks, but if wrecks there must be, please grant that they may be cast up on *our* shores. Amen.' As fate would have it, Neptune yielded up his namesake here on two occasions.

In April 1815 the brig *Neptune* of Fishguard was driven on shore near Godrevy, and as the crew struggled to get ashore, swarms of ruffians converged on the scene and proceeded to plunder whatever they could. Some of the rogues, who assembled under the pretence of protecting property from ruthless wreckers, had the audacity to relieve Captain Griffiths of his watch and snatch the crew's clothing, which they had retrieved at the risk of their lives. One seaman, who had got ashore half naked and who remonstrated with some miscreants for carrying off some rope, was told that unless he made an immediate departure and refrained from molesting them in securing their lawful spoil, they would strangle him forthwith.

Two years later the culm-carrying brig *Mary* of Ilfracombe stranded on these exposed Atlantic shores during the course of a strong northerly snowstorm. By a miracle of Providence, the whole crew was saved, and Captain James Bowden sought the help of local farmers and customs officers from St Ives in getting out the cables in an attempt to hold the ship in a position of safety. All that night and throughout the next day, teams of men were employed in securing the stores, carrying out their specialist tasks in an orderly and businesslike way. All went well until a rowdy party of Camborne miners arrived on the scene, wielding hatchets and threatening to murder anyone who got in their way, as they set about cutting the cables, plundering the stores and carrying off two small anchors. On the way home they had the gall, before darkness descended, to steal the shipwrecked seafarers' clothes, which kindly Gwithian folk had washed for them and hung out to dry. Captain Bowden, who owned the vessel and most of the cargo, which was uninsured, was almost ruined by this infamous behaviour, and there was some sense of poetic justice when the ringleaders were subsequently rounded up and committed for trial at the Assizes.

On one occasion (so the story goes) there was great competition amongst the skilful and daring pilots of St Ives to race their gigs out to a foreign vessel which had been sighted in the offing, displaying a light over her bows. Those who had been the first to spot the ship threw off their jackets, made a rapid launch, and pulled together in powerful, practised style, effectively outstripping all their rivals. As they neared the object of their desires, the helmsman called out, 'Stand ready to board her!' and the bowman shipped his oar, stood on the forethwart and made to grab her bulwarks in readiness to leap aboard. But there was nothing there! He toppled, and would have fallen headlong into the water, had not he been grasped by one of his mates and hauled back into the safety of the gig. Everyone was amazed, for the ship and its lights had just vanished into thin air. Could this phantom ship have been a premonition? For a sudden storm erupted, and next morning the barque *Neptune* of London was found wrecked on these shores, with the loss of all hands. All the victims, including Captain Grant and his son, were picked up shortly afterwards and now lie buried, along with countless other victims of shipwreck, in Gwithian churchyard. Not surprisingly, this reinforced a firmly held belief around these parts, that the appearance of phantom lights boded ill for mariners.

The shipwrecks continued with appalling regularity, and who can

Real wreck or phantom?

say how frequently phantom lights foretold their cruel fate? Did they shine forth on that last, fateful day of November in 1854, when the British India Steamship Company's vessel *Nile* went down with the loss of all hands? What had caused her to go off course by some 18 or 20 miles, when she had apparently been successful in weathering a severe storm, only to become another victim of The Stones? Strange tales emerged about intended passengers being delayed in Liverpool and thus avoiding a tragic fate, not to mention young Mr Strick from Newlyn, who put his bags aboard and went to have a quick pint with a friend, and did not know how lucky he was when he returned to the quay and saw his ship, containing all his luggage, steaming off to disaster.

Old customs die hard, for this dead wreck soon became the focus of the light-fingered, strong-fisted fraternity, who came loping down to the shore. Most of the wreckage came ashore between Portreath and Gwithian. As growing numbers of sightseers lined the cliffs, the more adventurous were down on the beach; some helping themselves to souvenirs, piling up large pieces of wood as spoil, or making off with more substantial prizes. One man shouldered a deck brush, another a ship's fender and a third had secured gratings from two of the ship's boats, which had washed ashore under St Mary's Well. A more ambitious character had descended a steep cliff by means of a rope, hoping to get his hands on the kegs, trunks and other items of cargo, which had been grouped together by the authorities, and placed above the waterline. But he was unable to haul any of it up the cliff, so there it had to remain until such time as calmer weather allowed it to be retrieved by boat. As darkness fell, one of the ill-fated vessel's masts was seen rolling pathetically in the surf, on that tragic and opportunist night.

Although shipwrecks in Cornwall were still quite numerous, and the heroic deeds of lifeboatmen had long since atoned for earlier tales of ruthless wreckers luring ships to their doom by displaying false lights, this particular incident achieved nationwide notoriety on account of being highlighted in *The Daily News*. This up-country newspaper broadly charged the Cornish with practising all the atrocities of wreckers, which, it claimed, most people in the rest of the country then regarded as a thing of the past. It went on to say that it was melancholy to reflect that, to the Cornish labourer on the coast, one of the commandments was rubbed clean out of the Decalogue. Warming to the theme, the writer went on to say, 'We talk of missionaries to the heathen. Is there one place that we can name where a mission is needed more than in Cornwall?'

Those sweeping statements drew forth a variety of reactions from the Cornish, who did not all wish to be tarred with the same brush.

Impromptu local investigations by the *West Briton* newspaper suggested that most of the goods of any worth seen handled, by an informant, were honestly delivered to the agents for the vessel; that merely odds and ends, suitable only for firewood, and a number of inconsequential items, had been carried off by folk on the coast, who had been so unfairly accused. If anyone was to blame, it had to be the unruly miners of Camborne, but they had got away with very little on this occasion.

The Cornish Telegraph, which had reported that pipes of sherry, casks of oil, kegs of lard and a host of other items had been washed ashore, mostly at Porthtowan, and taken to Portreath, spoke of barbarism and 'three or four hundred vultures in human shape' still hovering around, and some stubborn characters from Camborne and Illogan who were likely to bring further discredit on the county. As far as the criticism went, part of the confusion of those who made it stemmed from a lack of understanding of this maritime county and its culture, and of the definition of the term 'wrecking'. For, as some local folk pointed out with indignation, 'We showed no false lights.' If a vessel were to be wrecked with all lives lost, or efforts had been made to save human life, then what remained was a godsend for the impoverished inhabitants of Cornwall. Half-starved labourers and miners, much in need of the wherewithal to feed and clothe their families were being criticised for emulating their superiors. Since time immemorial lords of the manor, landowners and people in positions of power, as well as the Crown, had vied with each other for the rights of shipwreck all around our coasts. Furthermore, the smug attitude of people in the prospering cities might have more to do with the lack of recent shipwrecks on their streets, than their superior moral standards. How many people, anywhere, could honestly say that if they found a handsome purse filled with sovereigns they would seek to restore it, rather than romp home in the excitement of reward and discovery, rejoicing that this was their lucky day? Having made all these points, *The Cornish Telegraph* concluded by saying that wrecking was indefensible, and must be detrimental to the fair fame of Cornishmen.

When all was said and done, the wreck of the splendid, recently constructed, fast, iron, passenger screw-steamer *Nile*, and the attendant publicity, focused attention on the need to erect a lighthouse at Godrevy. In the event, it was sited on Godrevy Island, and it came into operation in March 1859, thereby creating a reassuring light for mariners, with hopes of eclipsing those forbidding phantom lights for ever.

20

The Exploits of Dicky Kingcup

◆

In a waterside tavern in Fowey, a century ago, Old Bill, who had been a notorious smuggler in his day, was enjoying a pint or two and a yarn with some fresh-faced young fisherlads from along the coast. As one pint followed another, Old Bill grew reflective and his thoughts turned to the good old days, when he was in his prime. 'By gosh,' he said, 'life were tough around these parts when I were a lad, and 'twas tougher still afore that. I can remember the old boys of sixty or seventy year ago. They was a different breed. They used to tell tales told to 'em by their fathers an' gran'fathers afore that, when smugglin' were in its 'eyday. But things is changin'; things is goin' soft. Sails givin' way to steam, pilots needin' certificates, an' that. You young 'uns ain't got the "go" in 'e fer the smugglin' business. Fishermen 'ave gone too 'spectable these days, I s'pose.' 'You can't turn back the clock,' observed young Tom. 'It's not that we are incapable of doin' these things,' pointed out young Denzil, 'For fishin' is as 'azardous as it ever were. 'Tis that we don't 'ave quite the same opportunities. Smugglin' days an' smugglin' ways 'ave gone for ever, more's the pity.' 'Tell us about the good ole days,' said Tom, attending to Old Bill's empty tankard.

'It were a great fraternity in they days,' declared Old Bill, settling back in his favourite bench in the corner, beside a blazing log fire. 'A jolly lot o' chaps they was, too, although 'tis true things did get a bit over'eated once or twice, wi' pistols an' fisticuffs an' that. Parsons was very different back-along; in the thick o' it, quite often. But then, all kinds o' folk was involved all along the line. 'Twere a regular industry. They were the days, to be sure, when good, pure sperrits was within the grasp o' every poor man!

'Ole Dicky Kingcup, 'e were a proper smuggler, 'e were, an' no mistake. Why, there weren't a keener smuggler on the ole coast than ole Dicky, rest 'is soul. 'Is fam'ly came from over Yealm way. 'E 'ad a brother called Phil wot was in free-tradin', too, but not a patch on 'im, an' another brother wot was an admiral. Well, Dicky, 'e joined the Coastguard over Polruan around about 1824, it must o' bin. But 'e only lasted about four year, afore 'e were kicked out. 'E weren't the first, nor the last, to be dismissed from the service for 'untin' wi' the 'ounds an' runnin' wi' the 'are. 'Is time in the Coastguard were a sort o' apprenticeship for 'is true vocation, which were smugglin'. 'Twere the very best apprenticeship 'e could ever 'ave 'ad. 'Twere valuable experience seein' thin's from the inside, knowin' their routines an' understandin' the way wot their minds worked. Mind you, even when 'e were a preventive man, 'e'd spend most of 'is time at the old Ship Inn. All the coastguards was expected to keep an eye on thin's after dark, but 'e never went out at night patter-rollin' along the coast, not Dicky Kingcup, not for anybody. 'E used ter say as 'ow 'e'd quit the coastguard on account o' seein' no future in it, no promotion. Be that as it may, 'e were less likely to end up a bullet through 'is 'ead as a smuggler, than as a coastguard.

'I first got to know Dicky after 'e left the Coastguard. 'E used ter be very thick wi' the smugglers afore 'e left the Coastguard 'ere in Fowey. But the authorities, they watched 'im pretty close. They know'd wot ole Dicky were up to, all right, Maybe it paid 'em to jus' keep an eye on 'im, for the company 'e kep'. For birds o' a feather, flock together. After 'e'd ducked 'is job at the Coastguard, 'e set up in a pub on the quay 'ere in Fowey, an' called it the Crown an' Anchor. That name showed 'is sense o' humour, too, followin' 'is 'unt wi' the 'ounds an' run wi' the 'are way o' thinkin'. Official soundin' like, an' respectable. Fingers in all kinds o' pies. Anyway, 'avin' 'is own pub were a crafty move. 'E knew where to get the finest sperrits, see, an' this were the perfect outlet for 'is ill-gotten gains, as you might say. No questions asked, no bother about movin' it on up the line, an' no need to give anyone else a cut o' the profits. 'Is beershop 'ere on the quay were an 'ive of industry. It were the place where you was sure ter meet up with various characters, if you get my meanin'.

'When 'e got into the big time, 'e wen' ter live down Plymouth, where 'e 'ad a lot o' good contacts. 'E 'ad the audacity ter set up as a shipbroker down Plymouth; a r'spectable callin' wot give 'im the perfec' cover for all 'is doubtful dealin's. An' 'e of'en came back 'ere to Fowey. E 'ad a perticuler sof' spot fer Fowey, where 'is career really go' started. Used ter say 'e were 'ere on business, inspectin' ships. 'E were 'ere on business, all right! All dolled up 'e were, jus' like an admiral's dinner. Funny thing about ole Dicky, although 'e'd lef' the Coastguard service, 'e never lost 'is taste for smart uniforms. P'raps it were on account of that brother, wot were an admiral. Anyway, 'e used to fair fancy 'isself struttin' around in this 'ere navy blue uniform wi' its shiny brass buttons, an' a peaked cap perched on 'is 'ead at a jaunty angle, like. Whenever 'e turned up, everybody would say, "Ah, ha! Watch out! Ole Dicky Kingcup's about!" If ole Dicky 'ad any weaknesses, they was vanity an' the growin' 'abit o' 'avin' one over the eight, specially when 'e grew older. Which reminds me, my tankard's runnin' dry.'

Old Bill's young companions took the hint, and asked him about the vessels involved in smuggling in those days. 'That's better,' he sighed, after taking another hearty swig or two and smacking his lips very loudly. 'Now, where was we?' 'You were goin' to tell us about some o' the vessels 'e used,' the youngsters reminded him. 'Oh, aye. Well, you can gen'r'ally reckon that any vessel as was mixed up in smugglin', 'e 'ad a 'and in it somewhere. You could bet yer ole sea boots on that. There was all kinds o' vessels an' all kinds o' places. 'Ere in Fowey there was the *Tam o' Shanter*, the *Jane* an' just about all the fishin' vessels at one time or another. But, like I said, after Dicky'd gone to Plymouth as a shipbroker, 'is work give 'im the perfect alibi. So 'e used a 'ole 'ost of vessels from near an' far, like the Cawsand galleys, the *'Enrietta* of Scilly, the *Two Brothers* of Plymouth and the trawler *Liberty* of Plymouth. 'E was well in wi' the French fraternity. Used a lot o' their smugglin' vessels, like the good ole *Le Oif*. Then there was the *Secret* of Poole, up Dorset way. Me ole brain's gettin' addled. Um . . . oh, yes. There was the ole *Four Brothers*, the *Good Intent*, the *Experiment*, the *Daniel an' William*, the *Providence an' Anne* . . . But the one wot means the most ter me were the dear ole *'Appy-go-Lucky*. An' she did live up to 'er name. We was 'appy in 'er, an' we was lucky . . .

'The very first business I were in wi' Dicky Kingcup were down the coast by Car'ayes. We'd bought an ole galley as 'ad once bin a preventive boat. 'Twas a notion wot appealed to ole Dicky; added a certain spice to things. So we called 'er the *'Appy-go-Lucky*. Fair 'andsome, she were. We used ter run a lot o' cargoes up on Port Luney beach. 'Twas the ideal place; no one much to bother us, an' 'andy for the Dodman. 'Twere a good enterprise. All went well until the day our luck ran out, when the *'Appy-go-Lucky* was seized on suspicion. She were taken to Falmouth an' cut up, so I do bel'eve. But she were pretty well worn out by then. She'd done a good turn, an' given us more than our money's worth.

'The first time I crossed the Channel wi' Dicky, were in the *Arethusa*, of Cawsand. She were about twenty ton, dandy-rigged, an' painted black, wi' tanned sails. On the way 'ome, we 'ad ter sink the goods off the Dodman. 'Tis a treacherous ole place, the Dodman, as many an unlucky seafarer do know to 'is cost. But the Gorran fishermen know'd it well, in all its moods. Know'd every nook an' cranny like the backs o' their 'ands. The idea were to get these Gorran crabbers to work the

Crabs and contraband dragged from the sea

goods for us, alongside liftin' their pots. The Gorran crabbers was in league wi' several o' the smugglers. We used ter place consignments on a sunken ledge just off the Dodman, to be 'arvested along wi' the crabpots. For 'oo could tell wi' the sharpest pair o' eyes, or even the most powerful spyglass, the difference atween fishermen raisin' their crabpots, an' fishermen bringin' up a few tubs at a time, which they 'id beneath those crabpots? An' if any nosy customs officers come sniffin' around, there's signals from the shore, an' the 'ole lot goes overboard. Terrible waste, but that didn't 'appen more'n a couple o' times. There was a power o' stuff brought ashore like that.

'So the first time we tries it out, we takes careful soundin's afore we puts the goods down, to make sure where this 'ere underwater ledge is to; the ledge where Gorran fishermen puts down their crabpots. 'Twas some tricky, for this 'ere ledge rises straight from the seabed, an' suddenly falls away into very deep water. So, like I said, we took careful soundin's, an' thought twelve fathoms were a nice depth o' water. But in the darkness o' the night, we 'ad sunk 'em much closer inshore than wot we thought. So when we begins to lift the tubs, we finds the bottom ran off to a great depth, an' most o' our 'ard won consignment 'ad bin swep' over the edge o' the rocks into deep water. 'Twas a fool's job. We only saved forty out o' the 'undred an' eight tubs wot we 'ad brought over. Must 'ave bin a fair lot o' intoxicated fishes swimmin' round about the Dodman after that! Round an' round in circles, I dare say! So we 'ad ter cut the drift line. It breaks me 'eart ter think about it, even now. That were a darned clumsy job, ter be sure. Then, as time went by, the coastguards got wise to this. Used to mess around off the Dodman wi' grappling irons, an' thought as 'ow clever they was when they 'ooked something up. Took it 'ome an' 'ad a good swig, I daresay! 'Twere top quality sperrits.

'Ole Dicky an' me, we crossed over to Roscoff a time or two. That were a fair ole toss, I can tell you! One time I recall I ventured twenty pound, an' 'e put in fifty. 'E weren't short o' a bob or two, even then. Anyway, we sink that lot off Portscatho beach, an' the 'ole operation went like a charm. Then there was the time Dicky was took, down at Par. Must've bin back in the eighteen forties. The young watchman, 'oo was the son of the chief boatman there see'd a spankin' new vessel, a schooner, she were, goin' into Par Bay. So this 'ere keen young watchman, 'e took a boat out an' boarded 'er. She didn't 'ave no licence, nor no number, this spankin' new vessel. "'Allo, Cap'n," says this 'ere young man, lookin' smart an' official like in 'is 'ansome new uniform. Then 'e see'd a man in the cabin, as looked as if 'e didn't want ter be seen. "An' 'oo is this 'ere?" 'e said. "Oh, 'im," says the Cap'n, lookin' all innocent, like. "'E's a man wot I brought around from Plymouth."

Puttin' 'is 'ead down an' lookin' inside the cabin, the young officer recognises the familiar face o' Dicky Kingcup. Just about everyone on the coast knew that face. "Oh Mr Kingcup, is that you?" says the young officer, boldly, like. "Oh, my!" 'e says (or words to that effect), "This is a bad job, to be sure." So the officer returns for 'is father an' another officer, called Mr 'Odge. They boarded the vessel, an' took 'er round to Fowey. None o' them would've bin sorry to see 'im locked up, for 'e gave the authorities more bother than anyone else on the 'ole coast. But they couldn't pin nothin' on 'im that time.'

There was a pause in the proceedings, while Old Bill stretched his legs and went to survey the twilit waterfront. 'Me an ole Dicky must've run 'undreds o' tubs up 'ere' said Old Bill, wallowing in nostalgia as he leant upon a wooden bollard on the quay and watched the movements of the vessels, with their lights reflected upon the water. 'Ole Dicky Kingcup an' all 'is associates must've run 'undreds an' undreds o' consignments up Fowey 'arbour, if the truth be known. 'E used ter 'ang about 'ere quite a lot, for 'e'd got consignments organised, partic'ly around Chris'mastide. There's many as would depend on Dicky to ensure a bountiful, merry Chris'mas, an' ole Dicky, bein' a man o' 'onour, as 'ow 'e saw 'isself, thought as 'ow it would've bin ungentlemanly to let 'em down.'

Back in the tavern, fortified by an enormous pasty, washed down with the right sort of lubricant, Old Bill was happy to continue his reminiscences, with an increasing number of listeners. 'Like I said, 'e 'ad a 'ole 'ost o' accomplices. Mixed up wi' characters like George Kirkin, 'Ambly, Cudlip, 'Icks o' Fowey, a chap o' the name o' Abraham summit, down Downderry, an' all the finest smugglers o' 'is day. 'E 'ad contacts at Los'withiel, up the river an' all around the bay. Pentewan, Mevagissey, Gorran 'Aven, Car'ayes, 'Emmick an' the Dodman; Falmouth, up the river and all around the creeks. But as time went by, 'e got more an' more involved to the east; Looe, Downderry, Cawsand, Plymouth an' the Yealm, where 'e 'ad 'ailed from.

''E nearly got 'is 'ands burnt back in thirty five, when 'e'd bin involved in a spot o' business wi' ole Thompson o' Los'withiel, in the *'Ope* o' Devonport. Thought 'e was smart wi' 'is crafty schemes, concealin' consignments in innocent-lookin' 'ay waggons an' the like. But this time the customs men 'ad the last laugh. They appeared from nowhere, an' suddenly pounced on the *'Ope*, when she were up the Yealm river. Started diggin', an' come across three 'undred an' seventeen tubs an' thirteen flagons, as just 'appened ter be concealed under a 'uge pile o' dung. 'E 'ad a job ter live that one down. Some'ow 'e managed ter wriggle out o' it, but 'e 'ad a job living ' that one down wi' the fraternity.

''Cos a lot o' farmers was in wi' it, too. Lot o' farmers out Lanreath way used ter be 'and in glove wi' Dicky Kingcup an' 'is merry men. They used to 'ide the kegs in their 'aylofts, an' some o' they labourin' lads fell wise to this. Used to borrow the keys an' go an' 'elp theirselves to a bit o' a tipple now and agen. You always know'd when they'd bin at it. They'd be drunk be'ind the plough, or staggerin' around all over the place, tryin' to drive the cattle 'ome. 'Twere a good job they thar cows knew wot they was at, or 'oo knows where they might've ended up!

'No one know'd Dicky Kingcup better than wot I did. Done a lot o' work together me an' Dicky. Like brothers, we was. But like I said, 'e 'ad two weaknesses. 'E were vain, an' 'e liked 'is sperrits too much. If 'e'd ever o' 'ad a downfall, 'twould 'ave bin on account o' the drink. Trouble was that when 'e 'ad access to all the sperrits wot 'is 'eart desired, 'e'd go chanterin' on, an' that was no good for business. 'E'd go chanterin' on, 'specially if there was a comely young maid around. We was always worried that 'e was goin' to let the cat out o' the bag. The most important thing about smugglin' was knowin' 'oo you could trust, an' keepin' mum about wot was 'appenin' along the coast. It was a case o' just mind no one's tale, but take care o' yoursel'. There was tales an' false tales. Red 'errings. You see, chaps might be pretendin' to tell you some secret, an' all the time they'd be lettin' you in. No, 'twas always safest to keep yer own counsel.

'Back in the ole days, aroun' eighteen fifty, there were a public 'ouse comin' up on the moor, on the road t' Lanreath. Used to be called The 'Atchet, but it were better known to one an' all as The Axe, on account o' the sign showin' an axe. Well, one night, after the goods 'ad bin landed at Looe, me an' Dicky was takin' a waggon load o' tubs inland, an' we was gettin' thirsty, like. So we pulled up outside the 'Atchet, to whet our whistles, like. But ole Dicky, 'e'd already bin busy whettin' 'is, wi' the result as wot 'e was 'alf seas over, as y'might say, afore the rest o' us 'ad a chance to mello' down a bit. Well, we got ter the bar room, an' 'e began a-shoutin' fer 'is liquor. So the lan'lord, 'e goes a rushin' around, while we jus' stands there, jus' knowin' that somethin' 'orrible was goin' ter 'appen. So when 'is drink were brought to 'im, 'e decided as wot it weren't to 'is likin'. So 'e flies into a terrible rage an' chucks it right across the bar-room; glass an' all. All this when we was carryin' a load o' cargo in a cartload o' dung, an' didn't want to attract no attention. But that's 'ow it were when 'e'd got the liquor inside o' 'im.

'Ole Dicky were sharp, but as the years went by an' the drink dulled 'is senses, 'e weren't always quite sharp enough. There were the time 'e were taken down on Lanivet beach, waitin' in a band o' smugglers for the boat to arrive from Roscoff. Ole Jenkins, the customs officer, 'e went up to old Dicky an' taps 'im on the shoulder, an' says. "I 'ereby arrest you in the Queen's name, Richard Kingcup," 'e says. So ole Dicky, 'e replies, "Well, Mr Jenkins, Sir, you'm the only man wot I'd ever allow to arrest me." Was 'e bein' stupid or was 'e smart? Maybe 'e was smarter than wot they thought. Word must've got around some'ow, for when the boat come in, there was no goods. So they couldn't arrest 'im for somethin' wot 'e'd not yet done. Kept everyone guessin', that time, 'e did. Kept everyone guessin', most times, really.'

'How was it with the revenue men and everyone knowing what he was really up to, that he didn't end up behind bars?' asked young Tom.

''E were too smart fer that. Up to every dodge 'e were. An' 'e 'ad charm. 'E could charm the birds out o' the trees, or the fishes out o' the ocean, could ole Dicky. 'E were a lovable rogue. Everyone liked ole Dicky. 'E were well in wi' the gentry. 'E 'ad the 'andy knack o' makin' everybody think 'e was one o' *them*. Whether it were rogues an' villains, cut-throats or 'eroes, sea cap'ns, merchants, magistrates or the gentry, 'e could talk their language. An' 'oo knows which side anyone's bread were buttered?' This brought forth a chuckle from Old Richard, who had just joined the party, who had served his time as a revenue cutter's man. 'I don't know about that,' he said, his eyes twinkling beneath his bushy eyebrows. 'But Ole Dicky Kingcup were a smart chap, an' no mistake. The Kingcups were relations o' ourn, an' the Admiral, who were Dicky's brother, an' my mother were very great friends. Brought up together as children. 'E were very fond of her. Used to call her Becky. He allus used to come and see her when he was 'ome from 'is voyages. 'E 'ad another brother, Phil, wot was also a great smuggler. But ole Dicky outshone 'im. Ole Dicky made this coast 'is very own!'

'I worked a time or two wi' Phil. 'E were a great smuggler, but 'e weren't in the same league as Dicky,' agreed Old Bill, who said he could pick out a family resemblance in the old revenue cutter's man. 'Phil, 'e lost 'is life when a Cawsand boat was wrecked off the Mewstone. 'Is 'ead was found arterwards in the cuddy o' the vessel. Three other men from Yealm was lost along wi' 'im, poor chap. But then, they weren't the only ones wot lost their lives over smugglin'; not by a long chalk. 'Twas a tough business. Specially the crossin' from Roscoff an' Cherbourg in the wintertime. It was sleet an' snow, an' blow, blow, blow! Fit enough to tear yer 'air out!

'Poor ole Phil Kingcup. I were comin' back from Cherbourg the night 'e were lost. Very stormy night, it were, 'though I've seen wuss. Wi' a donce o' a kick-up o' sea. We was goin' ter start together, but when we got underway, Phil sung out as they wouldn't be ready for another 'alf 'our or so. So they 'ad ter get their topsa'l down an' stowed. But arter a bit, we see'd them a-followin'. That were the last we ever see of the boat under sail. Next thing we knew was when she drifted on shore at

'Ope Cove, all 'er tubs 'ung round 'er, an' the ballast gone. The four bodies was seen lyin' on the bottom o' the sea, in clear, deep woter. They was masters o' the sea, but the last I ever seen o' Phil Kingcup an' 'is confederates was lyin' at the bottom o' the ocean. 'Twere the strangest sight wot I ever see'd.'

'What happened to Dicky Kingcup in the end?' asked young Denzil.

'Well, after 'e lost 'is brother 'e seemed ter fade away from the smugglin' scene o' 'is youthful exploits. P'raps 'e reckoned 'e'd made 'is fortune, pushed 'is luck far enough, an' decided ter quit when 'e was on top. 'E were an enigma; 'e were a paradox. All 'is life 'e'd kep' folk guessin'. In a way 'e 'ad the las' laugh on everyone. For after sailin' close ter the wind, an' a life o' jolly, rollickin' adventures, 'e didn't end up in Davy Jones' locker like 'is brother Phil, nor wi' a bullet shot through the 'ead. No. 'Twere a quiet, r'spectable kind o' passin'. 'E caught a cold at election time, an' died comfortable, in a feather-bed, me'be thirty or forty year ago. So dear Dicky Kingcup, as once wore a coastguard's button; Dicky Kingcup, the most notorious smuggler o' 'is day, 'e led a full an' 'appy life, God rest 'is soul.'

21

Accomplished with Oars

◆

'When you see a girl in a boat you may write her down "stranger", and if you see her handling a pair of sculls, you may be sure of it. The mothers of blue water men have as little as possible to do with the sea, and are content to admire its greens and blues shot with flaming sky tints, and dream of 'heavenly costumes' in like shades, at so much halfpenny per yard. Strong prejudices exist in places against woman being anything to do with boats; but custom differs greatly on the north and south coasts as to what women may or may not do, when men come ashore. That women and cats, hares and rabbits, bring 'bad luck' is a very general superstition; so a woman never goes out with her husband fishing, and seldom steps into a row boat.'
(Cornish Saints & Sinners: *J. Henry Harris*)

The sea is the mother of life and beauty, and the art of fishing is as old as humanity itself. For generations of Cornish fisherfolk, life revolved around fishing and boats, and the rhythms and vagaries of the ocean. Indeed, it has been said that when the fishermen were not out fishing, they were mending boats, painting boats, cleaning boats, or standing with their hands in their pockets gazing at boats. The seafaring sons of Cornwall were so much in harmony with their maritime environment, they thought of little else in their waking and sleeping hours, and took to the sea in their working boats for recreation. Thus the tradition of regattas evolved. Then, as now, they were rivals, pitting their skills against each other in deadly earnest while out on the water, but close comrades in the mellowing atmosphere of the tavern afterwards.

Every little fishing port around the long, indented coastline once had its own regatta, with specially devised races for the different categories of local and visiting craft. There was great excitement as the day of the regatta drew near, with streets and quaysides gaily festooned. Apart from the exciting spectacle out on the water, there was a host of attractions, providing fun and games for all the family on the shore, offering the welcome opportunity to cast care aside in those harsher times, with the rousing strains of local brass bands creating a jolly atmosphere.

Small regattas for the local population remained fairly low key, but towns such as Falmouth, St Mawes, Penzance, Newquay and Padstow sought to attract a wider following, as befitted their size and importance. The Newquay Regatta which took place on Midsummer Day in 1857 was an occasion which remained fondly in the memory of the thousands who attended. Folk started flocking into the town early in the morning, having travelled on foot, on horseback, or in a variety of conveyances, ranging from a donkey-cart to a grand four-in-hand. The arrival of the racing gigs from neighbouring towns, which were transported overland, brought an agreeable foretaste of the fun and excitement that was to follow. Meanwhile, a number of specially licensed booths were being erected on the Beacon, and stall holders set out tempting displays of cakes and candies, fruit and toys for the children. It was the magical, anticipatory calm before the junketing began in earnest.

Things really started to swing when the strident music of the Royal Miners' Artillery Band filled the air, and wafted across the water. A hurling match, played between Newquay and the parish of St Columb Minor, was won by Newquay, thanks to young Captain Osborne, who distinguished himself by being fleet o' foot. Although there were running matches, sports and a variety of hilarious diversions, such as climbing the greasy pole for a leg-o' mutton, all eyes were on the water at 3.30 pm, when six-oared gigs vied with each other over a seven-mile course, and the *Treffry* and *Dove* of Newquay, and the *Circe* of Truro emerged victorious. As there were a number of vessels in port at the time, a special event was arranged for ships' boats, over a distance of a mile and a half. There were a variety of other races, and the regatta concluded with an exciting gig and punt chase, just for the fun of it.

Each regatta had a spirit and following all of its own, and some, like the Royal Regatta, held at different venues were very splendid affairs indeed, with some events open to nationwide contestants, and a profusion of valuable prizes. The 'crack' Mount's Bay lug sail boats, the Cawsand yawls and the pilot boats all added to the stunning spectacle. By the middle of the last century, when lifeboats were being emplaced around the Cornish coast, the RNLI saw the potential of these prestigious events for giving lifeboats, and the Institution a higher profile, attracting more revenue, and lifeboat racing became very popular. Thus, new lifeboats arrived on station in a blaze of publicity, to the stirring strains of *See the Conquering Hero Comes*, with crews and craft being put through their paces, to the delight of one and all. Lifeboat races, which were contested in deadly earnest, sometimes

The Saltash maidens triumph again

erupted into fisticuffs when things got too passionate. It was disappointing when these popular events had to be phased out, for it was felt that the assembly of lifeboats in one place left whole sections of the coast vulnerable, should an emergency arise.

Strangely, in a county which discouraged the fair sex from messing about in boats, the most illustrious rower which Cornwall ever produced was a woman. This was the exception which proved the rule, and Anne Glanville's colourful lifestyle could only have evolved in Saltash, an ancient borough close to the Royal Naval base, in the idealistic age of the Jolly Jack Tar. Saltash (or Esse), which had been a thriving seaport and market long before Plymouth existed, had long-established traditions of ships and seafarers proudly serving the nation in a worldwide context, as well as rights of anchorage, ferrying and oyster-dredging. Thus, generations of sturdy Saltashers, born into these maritime traditions, gained their sea-legs before they could even walk on land. Necessity was the mother of invention, and local boatmen turned their skills to harnessing the immediate needs of trade and industry around them.

Anne, who was born into this tough, seafaring community in 1796, when women were engaged in shrimping, cockling, dragging for lug and long-lining, hawking fish around or hobbling, married a boatman and became part of the action, rowing her own boat here, there and everywhere, as needs dictated. It was customary for the brawny women of Saltash to carry vast quantities of cockles and mussels from Devonport to Plymouth every day, and the place became renowned for its accomplished boatwomen, as well as boatmen. Anne, who was to bear 14 children, and who took over as breadwinner for her large family when her husband became ill, was a tall, strapping lady, bright and cheerful, who found favour with royalty and eminent folk for her unaffected charm and zest for life. She was a much loved personality around the harbour, where she plied her boat and indulged in witty repartee with the sailors on the ships, who knew her affectionately as 'Mother'.

The rowers of Saltash were well known for their prowess with the oar; so much so that, in 1824, contestants in the Plymouth Regatta pulled out, because they did not wish to risk humiliation against the Saltash men. So, in the event, prizes to the value of £8 were offered in a four-oared race for women, and the ladies of Saltash emerged victorious. The idea caught on, and the ancient nautical borough of Saltash concentrated on its regattas, which became famous events. It was said that the ladies of Saltash feathered their oars with such dexterity that few of the opposite sex would compete against them. To add a touch of femininity to their Amazonian style, they took to wearing distinctive white attire, consisting of frilly caps, adorned with blue ribbons, and short, frilly nighties (with blue 'safeguards'), and cut a dash wherever they went. These tanned, sinewy ladies, who competed in events all over the country, achieved fame, and captured hearts, but none was more renowned than Anne Glanville, the leader of the crew, who always pulled on the 'stroke' oar. Indeed, it was said that for many years Anne enjoyed the reputation of being the champion female rower of the world.

In August 1842, *The West Briton* reported:

'On Saturday se'nnight, great interest was excited in Portsmouth, by the arrival of the celebrated Saltash crew, headed by the renowned Anne Glanville. We are informed that a match was made between Mr Waterman of Anderton, and the officers of the 36th Regiment, now stationed at Portsmouth, for the sum of £100, one boat to be rowed by the Saltash women, another by a like number of the above named officers. Immediately upon the arrival, the Saltashers went to work, and in a trial race with the women of Portsmouth, beat them by about three miles and a half. They next contended with some of the crack Dockyardsmen, whom they also beat by three boats' length – so that when they came to the starting boat, on Monday, the day appointed for the grand struggle, they were deprived of the further pleasure of beating the gentlemen antagonists, by the voluntary relinquishment of the bet. The fact is, they made such short work of their opponents on the previous Saturday, that the officers became frightened as to the result, and to be thrashed by women was a thing not to be endured.'

If this encounter brought satisfaction to the Saltash stalwarts, not to mention a few nods and winks and pithy comments in many a nautical tavern, the swiftly arranged trip across the Channel must have been relished by Anne and her colleagues for the rest of their days. Having just achieved such success at Portsmouth, the ladies went along with Captain Russell's suggestion to enter themselves for the stakes at the Havre Regatta, which was open to worldwide entrants, to 'take the shine off the Frenchmen' for 'the honour of Old England'. Put this way, it was a challenge they could not resist, so they left Plymouth aboard his ship HMS *Brunswick*. They were escorted into the town by bandsmen and the military, and were most politely received by the Mayor and his Committee, who did them the honour of drinking their health, shaking them by the hand and engaging them in conversation. But, as it transpired, some Frenchmen, like the Portsmouth heroes, not wishing to risk a defeat by women, and above all *Englishwomen*, declined the proposed encounter. However, alternative arrangements were smoothly put into operation.

If some had been inclined to mock, they had the smirks removed from their faces when 'les Anglaises de Saltash' had a brief limbering-up session to demonstrate their style, packed with power and ease and grace. Over ten boats took part in the four-oared gig event, when Captain Russell acted as their coxswain. They experienced rather an unfair start, which meant that six boats were ahead of them five minutes after the beginning of the race. 'Bend your backs to it, Maidens, and hoorah for Old England!' called Anne, defiantly. One by one, they managed to draw alongside, then overtake, each of their opponents, with an encouraging word from Anne. It was a long course, and a hard pull, but at length the Saltash maidens, with the British colours flying proudly at the fore, took the lead. They beat the opposition by at least 100 yards. They were well and truly thrashed, in front of 20,000 excited spectators. Thus it was that our celebrated Amazons, who joyfully accepted a new trophy on the bosom of the Seine, were given a spectacular send-off by delighted new admirers. 'Didn't us feel proud at that moment, and often afterwards,' said Anne in later years. 'For 'twas for the glory of Old England!'

Fashions in sport, like everything else, tend to come and go in cycles. By the end of the last century the Saltash women were not really interested in rowing in regattas. But now rowing and gig-racing is enjoying an enthusiastic revival, in the Isles of Scilly and all around the coast of Cornwall, with other events being organised much further afield.

22

Power and Piracy

◆

The isolated and exposed Cornish peninsula has always attracted the attentions of adventurers who came to conquer, steal and plunder. In the early 10th century savage Danish pirates infested every part of the coast, landing unexpectedly by day or night, and laying the land to waste with fire and sword. They penetrated inland, burning villages, plundering churches, slaughtering the inhabitants and disappearing rapidly over the horizon, heavily laden with gold, silver, cattle and other ill-gotten gains.

In the course of the on-going power game over the centuries, there have been countless bloody skirmishes enacted off these shores, particularly with the French and the Spaniards. At the time of the Spanish wars it was a favourite ploy to carry off innocent fishermen, who would be interrogated about shipbuilding activities and the strength of the English fleet. Whether in peace-time or in war, the coastal population could never sleep easily in their beds at night, for fear of marauders of one sort or another. In the 17th century it was the dreaded Turkish pirates, who were actually from Tunis, Tripoli, Sallee (Sale) and Algiers, along the Barbary coast. The very sight of these swarthy villains, with dark, flashing eyes, in their colourful shirts, tarbooshes, baggy pantaloons and wide cummerbunds bulging with weapons, was enough to strike terror in the hearts of anyone who beheld them. But heaven help those who stood in their way as the blood-curdling war-cries rose to a climax, with the flourishing of their sharp, flashing scimitars and the threat of their loaded pistols. These ruthless Barbary pirates plundered, raped and murdered, captured prize ships and their crews, and carried off local fishermen to be sold into slavery on the Barbary coast.

If the maritime county of Cornwall has produced a colourful variety of valiant seafaring heroes and villains, it is not always easy to distinguish one from the other, for definitions would depend on the attitudes of the time, and whose side they were on. When the storm clouds of the Spanish Armada were brewing over the realm, piracy was rife, for the attacking of foreign vessels not only weakened the power of Spain and other foreign countries, it also sharpened the skills of the sailors of the west, to be employed in earnest in maritime warfare. Privateering, which required letters of marque or other official documentation, was artfully encouraged by the Queen, and this gave rise to many swashbuckling deeds. Privateering spilled over into free-lance piracy, also known as freetrading or freebooting, and into slickly organised smuggling. Indeed, the situation was so complex that it was suggested that certain high ranking Cornish families, who had acquired wealth, power and status by their prowess in battle and sophistication in piratical exploits, were double agents, secretly capitalising on the activities of the corsairs, which were foreign privateers who might or might not be licensed. Strange dealings occurred in December 1562, when a corsair, commanded by a notorious Frenchman known to one and all as Old Timber Toes, sailed from Havre and, after capturing Portuguese and Biscayan vessels, drove a Spanish ship ashore in Falmouth harbour. When the indignant Spanish captain appealed to the governor of Pendennis Castle, he was told that the privateer's documents were in order, and nothing could be done about it without special permission from the Queen. Shortly afterwards Old Timber Toes increased his assets still further, by seizing some Portuguese vessels that had sought refuge here.

During the reigns of Henry VIII and Edward, the seafarers of Cornwall and Devon formed themselves into a fleet of privateers, and became known as 'The Adventurers of the West'. The Cornish ports supplied men and ships, and the combined fleet of 30 or 40 sail must have created a magnificent spectacle and provided a formidable backing for the Royal Squadron. The leading families of Edgcumbe, Arundell, Denzel, Moyle, Grenville and Godolphin were among the notable western worthies. There had long been a need for more efficient coastal fortifications, as this letter from John Arundell of Trerice to Thomas Cromwell, written around 1537, demonstrates:

'There came into Falmouth haven a fleet of Spaniards, and the day after came four ships of Dieppe, men-of-war, and the Spaniards shot into the Frenchmen, and the Frenchmen shot into the Spaniards, and during three hours great guns shot between them, and the Frenchmen were glad to come higher up the haven; and the morrow after St Paul's day the Spaniards came up to assault the Frenchmen, and the Frenchmen came up almost to the town of Truro and went aground there. I went to the admiral of the Spaniards and commanded him to keep the king's peace and not to follow further; but the Spaniards would not, but said, "I will have them or I will die for it." And then the Spaniards put their ordnance in their boats, and shot the French admiral forty or sixty shots during a long hour, the gentlemen of the city, Mr Killigrew and Mr Trefusis and others, taking pleasure at it. Then I went to the Spaniards and told them to leave their shooting, or I would raise the country upon them. And so the Spaniards left. My lord, I and all the country will desire the king's grace that we may have blockhouses made upon our haven.'

Fortifications were emplaced at Falmouth, St Mawes, Fowey and other places around the coast in the time of Henry VIII. Pendennis Castle was built on the site of an ancient fortification, and John Killigrew, Esq., on whose land the castle was first erected, was appointed the first governor.

The powerful and influential Killigrew family, mentioned here, and who dwelt at Arwenack on the shores of Falmouth haven, were a law unto themselves. Having acquired the manor of Arwenack by marriage to an heiress, they established a house here, which came to be regarded as one of the finest and most costly mansions in Cornwall. It was the Killigrew family who initially saw the potential of Falmouth as an important seaport; a vision which eventually led to its golden age as a Post Office Packet port. This adventurous family possessed a strange blend of qualities which were necessary to achieve power and eminence in those brutal days. As well as being brave, gallant, stylish and extravagant, they were also somewhat dissolute, artful and addicted to piracy. For they possessed a love of sailing close to the wind and the excitement of intrigue. But, if certain members of the family were keen to demonstrate their prowess in those swashbuckling days, the most dastardly deed around these parts was perpetrated by a petticoat pirate.

There are a number of variations to this tale, which was briefly documented but coloured up over the centuries. The popular story goes that, on New Year's Day in 1582, a rather battered Dutch vessel, heavily laden with valuable merchandise, under the ownership of the Spaniards, sailed into Falmouth harbour to seek refuge from the terrible storm which had been raging for some days. She came to anchor within the Bar, opposite Arwenack House, and, thankful to have reached a safe haven at last, her Spanish owners Juan de Chaves and Philip de Oryo, who was also the captain, came ashore to seek the comforts of a local inn. It just so happened that Lady Jane (some sources say Dame Mary) Killigrew, who was sitting by the casement, cast languid eyes across the troubled water, and caught sight of the vessel as it came to anchor so obligingly near to her home. This was an opportunity not to be missed, and lassitude and boredom soon gave way to swift and reckless action.

Lady Jane leads the attack

The peace of that Sabbath day was shattered as the doughty dame summoned her servants and instructed them to prepare a boat, for, in the absence of her husband, she instructed them to go aboard the foreign vessel to ascertain the nature of its business. Then she swore them to secrecy about the conspiracy. So a boat was duly dispatched, and her closest confederates, Kendall and Hawkins, returned with the desirable news that she was, indeed, laden with treasure; that the owners were enjoying the luxury of being ashore until repairs had been carried out and that the vessel was in the charge of two Spanish agents and a token Dutch crew. This fulfilled her most optimistic hopes, and excitement rose as the wicked plotters worked out their evil strategy. Initially, Lady Jane proposed that they should return to the ship and either appropriate its valuable cargo by force, or exact a large sum of money from the crew in lieu of plunder, and for deliverance from death. Then, as excitement mounted, Lady Jane decided that she wanted to be part of the action herself, and they all relished the excitement.

Sounds of foreboding must have reverberated around the harbour over the next few hours as Lady Jane assembled a motley band of cut throats and villains to assist her in her ruthless intentions. They contained themselves until the midnight hour before striking. Then came a loud cheer, as the largest boat in the harbour, crammed with ruffians armed with pikes, swords and daggers, left the shore, under the direction of the formidable Lady Jane, who stood tall and statuesque in the stern, on this sinister, moonlit night. As they drew alongside the vessel, the pirates leapt over the gunwales, swarmed across the decks and threatened the startled sailors with instant death if they dared to make an outcry.

The Dutch crew, taken by surprise, were soon overpowered and tied to the masts and stanchions. But the Spaniards, despite all the odds, tried to resist and promptly paid for it with their lives, with their bodies being unceremoniously flung overboard. In the course of the struggle, one of the Spanish factors, who had found pause to pray for his soul, also uttered a curse on the male heirs of the evil Lady Jane, which came home to roost in due course. In domesticity, politics and war they seemed jinxed, and eventually the family became extinct. Having ransacked the ship and helped themselves to anything which took their fancy, including two hogsheads of Spanish pieces-of-eight, sundry bolts of hollands and bales of high quality leather, they got the plunder ashore, and set sail for Ballentynmoor, in Ireland, to give the vessel a more thorough going-over. After all the risk and excitement, the headstrong Lady Jane was disappointed that she had not secured a more valuable loot, and petulantly laid claim to most of the maid's share (the percentage traditionally given to the servants). She buried the plunder in the garden, fearing that her husband might discover her terrible secret. For, as she warned her conspirators, if he were to find out they might all be hanged.

Even in those lawless times these capers caused quite a scandal. Furthermore, it was quite a coincidence that twelve of the Killigrew servants had gone missing at just the time the vessel had been whisked away to Ireland; a situation that Sir John Killigrew found hard to explain away. This was particularly embarrassing as he held the responsible position of Commissioner of Piracy at the time. Not surprisingly suspicion fell heavily on Kendall and Hawkins, but they were let off the hook on account of an alibi provided by one Elizabeth Bowden, an obliging landlady who kept a small inn at Penryn. She swore that they were there at the time the offence was committed, and the jury returned an open verdict that the vessel had been stolen by persons unknown. But Juan de Chaves and Philip de Oryo, the owners of the vessel, were not content to let the matter rest there and lodged a complaint with a higher authority in London. The Earl of Bedford instructed Sir Richard Grenville and Mr Edmond Tremayne to make searching investigations, and thus the whole truth eventually came to light

Lady Killigrew, Kendall and Hawkins were sent for trial at Launceston Assizes, and all three were duly found guilty and sentenced to death. However, Sir John obtained the influential support of Sir John Arundell and Sir Nicholas Hals, and Queen Elizabeth was induced to grant a pardon for Lady Jane. When the news of this unequal justice reached the ears of her partners in crime, their chief regret was that they were to be deprived of the company of 'old Jezebel Jane' at the gallows, and roundly cursed her and everyone involved in procuring her pardon. Thus the men were executed on the walls of Launceston Castle, while the arch-villainess of this diabolical affair escaped the noose.

Acknowledgements

I should like to thank the many people who have helped me in researching this book, and in particular:

Jack Snell, for many happy hours of yarning, and researching material for 'Jack and the *Jean Charcot*'. William Parker of the Lifeboat Enthusiasts' Society, for substantial help in researching 'The Drama of the *Flying Enterprise*'. David Wilkinson of the Lifeboat Enthusiasts' Society, for his help and interest, particularly in regard to 'An Epic Lifeboat Service'. Kevin Heath, for his help in researching 'Two Sail Standing Out'. Catherine Vinot, for French translation. Anne-Mieke Chandler, for Dutch translation. Stephen Pellow and G.C. Fox & Co., Shipping Agents, Falmouth. Kate Richards. Tony Warren. Jimmy Morrison. Kevin Hanlon. Terry, Kim and Joanne, of the Local Studies Library, Redruth. Hodder and Stoughton for permission to use an extract from Arthur Mee's *The King's England – Cornwall* (1937).

I am also indebted to: Falmouth Library. Plymouth Library. Public Records Office, Kew. Greenwich Maritime Museum. RNLI. Lifeboat Enthusiasts' Society. Société Nationale de Sauvetage en Mer. Dutch Lifeboat Service. *Great Britain's Coasting Pylot,* 1693, Captain Greenvile Collins. *Cornish Shipwrecks*, Frank Strike. *The Life-Boat. The Lizard Lifeboats Centenary Year 1859-1959* by F.G. Chapman. The Log of the *Mystery. The Story of Padstow's Lifeboats 1827-1977* by Claude Berry. *Lloyd's Weekly* Casualty Reports. *Falmouth Packet. Cornish Guardian. The Cornishman. Cornish & Devon Post. The Times. Daily Telegraph. Western Morning News.* And last, but certainly not least, Jenny Fryatt for her superb illustrations.